• David Easter • John Eaton • Rita Eaton • Forrest Eber • Santiago Echeverri • Neil Eckardt • Kerilee Eddy [illegible]a • Heather Edick • Slivy Edmonds Cotton • Christopher Edwards • David Edwards • Morris Effron • [illegible]rg • Diane Einsele • Andrew Eisenberg • Peter Ekman • Carl Ekstrom • Josh Eliashberg • Amaranath [illegible]on Ellsworth • Michael Ellyatt • gregory elmiger • rw emeigh • Dale Emerson • Mia Encarnacion • Ma[illegible] • Kiran Epari • Steve Epner • David Epstein • steve epstein • Pablo Erat • Zoli Erdos • Alexandra Eremia • [illegible]man Ernst • Jim Eromin • Kevin Ertell • Rico Escalante • Dave Esler • Alfred Essa • robert esser jr. • [illegible] • jeremy ettinghausen • Antoine Eustache • Antoine Eustache • Ben Evans • Glenn Evans • John Evans • Lilly Evans • Lilly [illegible] • Philip Evans • Roger Evans • Nathan Everett • Pamela Evers • Larry Everson • Max Evett • Andy F • gianandrea facchini • Brian Fadel • Peter Fader • Mohammed Faifi • Antonio Faillace • Harold Falber • Dietrich Falkenthal • Amy Fandrei • Chris Fanini • Jolanda Fannin • William Farancz • Tássilu Faria • Timothy Farnham • Kate Farrell • Dana Farver • Ross Fattori • Grant Fawcett • Justin Fawson • Mark Fedorov • Hank Feeser • Stephen Fefferman • eleanor feit • John Felan • Rich Feller • Wei Feng • Nigel Fenwick • Thierry Ferey • Craig Ferguson • Marcelo Fernandes • David Fernandez • Oliver Fernandez • Rolly Ferolino • Jim Ferrans • Margaret Ferraro • William Ferris • Kristine Ferry • Loraine Fick • Thad Fidler • Kevin Fielder • Clive Findlay • Charles Fine • michal fineman • Barbara Finer • Tim Finin • Shane Finlay • fatima firoozi • Beth Fischer • Danny Fischer • Heiko Fischer • Randal Fischer • Roger Fischer • Shira Fischer • Daniel Fischmar • Guy Fish • Denise Fisher • Donald Fisher • Jackie Fisher • Teddi Fishman • Rosanna Fiske • Eric Fitz • Margaret Fitzgerald • Rob Fitzgibbon • Shelley Fitzmaurice • Bob Fitzpatrick • Christine Fitzpatrick • Sebastian Fixson • Sara Flaherty • danny flamberg • Scott Flaming • Daniel Fleder • Dick Fleissner • Bruce Fleming • Adam Fletcher • Chris Fletcher • Rob Flickenger • Keely Flint • Chris Flohre • Scott Flora • Mónica Flores • Raul (Rudy) "Flores, Jr." • Doug Floyd • Joseph Flumerfelt • Terence (Terry) Flynn • Brad Focht • Philip Foeckler • Mat Fogarty • Tom Fogarty • Jay Fogelman • Kevin Foley • Richard Foley • James Folkestad • Bruno Fonte • scott forcino • scott forcino • Eric Ford • Daniel Forester • Mark Fortier • ronald fortune • Sarah Foster • Mark Fournier • Melanie Fournier • Heather Fox • Wayne Fox • DARYL FOY • Eugene Frame • Tim France • James Francey • Marcelo Franco • Linda Frank • Steve Frank • Marc Frankel • John Franklin • Carl Frappaolo • Stephen Fraser • Kevin Frazier • Ronald Frazier • Magnus Fredriksson • Robert Freed • David Freedman • Mary Freeman • Terry Freeman • Mark Freiheit • Josue Freitas • Kevin Freitas • Paul French • Benjamin Frenkel • Lorenzo Freschet • Kelly Frey • stu friedman • jim fries • Bertrand Friot • frombegin frombegin • Douglas Frosst • Andy Frost • Graeme Frost • Kelvin Fu • Miguel Fuentes • Gerry Fulbrook • Edward Fuller • Mary Ellen Fullhart • James Fulop • Mei Lin Fung • Bob Furst • Roberta Fusaro • Chris Fusco • Grzegorz Futa • Hugo Fuxa • Ashutosh G • Balasubramanian G • Narasimhan G • Rajagopal g • Aloysius Gabriel • Rony Gabriel • Christine Gaca • Gary Gaddy • Chris Gadient • Nikhil Gadre • Dan Gagne • Pierre Gagnier • Larry Gagnon • Jay Gaines • Michael Gaio • Ashok Gairola • Oliver Gajda • Aniket Gajendragadkar • Creative Gal • Emi Gal • manuel galas • Diane Galbraith • Marc Galin • Gerald Gallagher • Chris Galloway • James Gamage • Priyanka Gambhir • Julia Gamburg • ellen gamerman • Sunita Ganesan • Deepjyoti Ganguly • Robi Ganguly • Stuart Gannes • maisie ganzler • Avtandil Garakanidze • Juan Bau Garcia • Linda Garcia • Maria Garcia • Martin Garcia • Daniel García De Weert • Igor García Olaizola • Miguel Garcia-Gosalvez • Adrian Gardiner • Michelle Gardner • Manish Garg • Kiran Garimella • Mia Garlick • Spencer Garner • Norman Garrett • Rosalie Garrett • Lucy Garrick • Eric Garulay • Erica Garvey • Jerry Gasche • Scott Gast • Michael Gat • Steven Gates • Gina Gaudio-Graves • Saurabh Gautam • Marina Gavrilova • Eugene Gaysinskiy • Joseph Geary • Dorit Geifman • Jeff Geiser • Christi Gell • David Gelman • Richard Gentry • Samuel George • Sean Georges • Ed Geraghty • Marla Gerein • Lorne Gerlach • Scott Germaise • John Gerome • Joe Gerstandt • Marc Gerstein • John Gerstner • Hans Gerwitz • Mary Ghikas • salil ghosh • sayan ghosh • MICHAEL GIANNAKIS • Philip Gibbs • Paul Gibler • Deborah Gibson • George Gibson • George Gibson • Stuart Gibson • William Gienke • Fabio Giglietto • Lisa Gilbert • Bob Gilbreath • Harold Gill • Shoaib Gill • Jay Gillan • Kathy Gillen • craig gillespie • Peter Gillespie • Thomas Gilmartin Jr. • Matthew Gilmore • Bryan Gilpin • Kathleen Gilroy • Henner Gimpel • Gail Ginther • Ricardo Gioia • Tanya Giovacchini • Angela Githuthu • Elizabeth Giuliani • Amrithaa GK • Gerry Gleason • gustavo glibota • Elizabeth Glick • Whitney Glockner • Peter Gloor • Suzann Gobis • Frederic Godart • Javier Godoy • Abhinav Goel • Anuj Goel • deepak goel • Andreas Goeldi • Mike Goetter • Jarrett Goetz • Thomas Goetz • Kathe Gogolewski • Eric Goh • Pierre GOIRAND • A. Nesrin Goker • YVONNE GOLASZEWSKI • Alex Golberg • Anna Gold • Alon Goldberg • Jeff Goldberg • Carole Goldin • Graham Golding • Arnie Goldman • Kyle Goldman • Laurie Goldman • Mort Goldman • Deborah Goldring • Eli Goldstein • Jonathan Goldstein • Carlos Gomes • Juan Carlos Gomez Sanchez • Amelita Gonzales • Alberto Gonzalez • Jose-Gregorio Gonzalez • Martin Gonzalez • Nestor Gonzalez • Reynaldo Gonzalez • Carlos González Mozuelos • JoAnn Gonzalez-Major • Gustavo Gonzalez-Sanchez • John Gooden • jenny goodman • arnold goodwin • liz gooster • Devika Gopal • Sri Gopalan • Jean Gora • Nikolai Gorchilov • Jennifer Gordon • Jonathan Gordon-Till • Jill Gorman • Rick Gormley • Anuj Gosalia • francois gossieaux • Mike Gotta • Linda Gottschalk • Tasi Gottschlag • Paul Goulding • Pascal Goursaud • Cristina Gouveia • Philip Graber Graber • Mark Grabowski • Andreas Graef • Jay Graff • Ann Graham • CHARLES B. GRAMP • Suresh Grandhi • Alan Grant • Christopher Grant • robert grant • David Granville • Ellwood Gray • Joe Greco • Bradly Green • Charles Green • Denise Green • Paul Greenberg • John Greene • jean greenland • Howard Greenstein • Toni Greenwell • Lewis Greer • Hal Gregersen • andrea gregoris • John Gregory • Storm Gregory • Amy Gretz • Hugh Grey • Jennifer Greyling • Matt Griffin • Andrew Griffiths • Kathie Grigg • Jennifer Griggs • Dan Grigorovici • Catherine Grimes • Jeff Grimshaw • Gregory Grinberg • Brian Grinder • Francesca Grippa • Jerrold Grochow • Daniel Gronowski • Steffi Groppe • Char Lyn Grujoski • Lisa Grunberger • Bin Gu • Sudhakar Gudlannagari • Ingrid Guerra-Lopez • Daniel Guerrero • Esteban Guerrero • PAUL GUETTER • deepanjan guha • Richard Guha • Didier Peter Guillemard • Hardeep Gulati • daniel gullett • Mohan Gundu • Dale Gundy • eileen gunn • Paul Gunther • Robert Gunther • Debbie Gunzelman • Ching Guo • Amit Gupta • anu gupta • Arun Gupta • Ashish Gupta • Kalyan Gupta • Malvika Gupta • Priya Gupta • Sachin Gupta • Sandeep Gupta • SAURABH GUPTA • Sumit Gupta • Suraj Gupta • Uma Gupta • Varun Gupta • Vivek Gupta • Gouri Gupte • Janet Guptill • Grzegorz Gurgul • Edward Gurowitz • Santhosh Guru • Santosh Gurubasannavar • Alex Gururajan • Muthuraj Guruswamy • Ellina Gurvits • John Gutheil • Francisco Gutierrez • Sergio Gutiérrez • Jose Guzman • ronald guzman • steve guzman • Rick Guzzo • Hans Henrik H. Heming • Thomas Haadsma • Vanessa Haakenson • Michael Hackard • Lee Hadaway • Wilson Haddow • Andrew Haeg • Carolin Haeussler • Leigh Hafrey • chris hagenbuch • Elisabeth Hager • Jesse Hager • Jaafer Haidar • Jan Haig • cyril haioun • Aric Haley • jay haley • Teddy Halim • George Halkias • Janet Hall • Melvin Hall • Su Hallenbeck • susan halligan • Erika Halloran • Erika Halloran • Richard Halloran • Erika2 Halloran2 • Andrew Hallowell • Bob Halperin • Myles Halsband • Edvard Halupa • Michael Hamer • Jo Hamill • Scott Hamilton • Kaliya Hamlin • Steven Hammersly • Brett Hammond • James Hampton • Sherif Hanala • Pablo Handler • Carl Hanks • Mike Hanlon • neal hannon • Deren Hansen • Garron Hansen • Mark Hanson • Wayne Hao • Charles Harbour • michelle hardy • Rob Hardy • Richard Hare • Amanda Hargis • miguel harik benitez • Peter Harkes • Chris Harley-Martin • Richard Harmer • Rainer Harms • Grady Harp • Stephen Harper • Steve Harrell • Marti Harrington • Mary Harrington • Casey Harris • Jason Harris • Laura Harris • BRUCE HARRISON • Chad Harrison • Suzanne Harrison • Jean Hart • riad hartani • Timothy Hartge • Merle Harton • Jamal Hashim • Shimon Hason • tim hassed • Hunter Hastings • Patrice Hatcher • Emmanuel Haton • Frances Haugen • Matthew Haugh • tom haughton • Sascha Häusler • Robert Hawkins • David Hawthorne • michael hawtin • Claudio Hayashi • yoshito hayashi • Marguerite Hayden • Charlene Moore Hayes • Heidi Hayes • Annie Miu Hayward • Bruce Hazard • Isaac Hazard • Norm Healey • Bruce Hecht • Rich Hecker • William Hederman • Kathryn Hedgepeth • Alan Heffner • Arnold Heggestad • Mia Hegnhøj • Gregory Heim • Christine Heinsohn • Matthew Helbig • Tamara Helenius • Elaine Helle • Wolfgang Heller • Thomas Hemingway • Jay Hemmady • Colin Henderson • Lee Henderson • Patricia Henderson • Ronald Lee Henderson • Vani Henderson • Brad Hendricks • Neal Hendrickson • Laurie Henneborn • Rob Hennigar • Mark Henricks • bob henry • richard henry • Paul Hensel • David Henson • Quinn Heraty • daniel herb • scott herman • William Hermanek • Antti Hermunen • Ania Hernandez • LEOVINO HERNANDEZ • Manny Hernandez • Michael Hernandez • Xavier Hernandez • Leanne Herne • Carlos Herreros • Ann Herrmann • Robert Hess • Reid Hester • Alex Hewitt • Gregory Hewko • Greg Heyes • Karen Hibbard • Martin Hickey • James Hicks • Diego Hidalgo • Jose Luis Hidalgo • Carrie Higbie • Craig Higdon • jeremy hight • Alexander Hill • cindy hill • Graham Hill • TRACY HILL • Rob Hilliard • Steve Hiltunen • Peter Himler • Patrick Hindert • dwight hines • Pete Hines • James Hipps • Ronald Hirasawa • Takashi Hirayama • Arnold Hirshon • Jason Hitchings • Penny Hix • Angie Ho • Andy Hobsbawm • Jonathan Hochman • Rasmus Hoejengaard • Eric Hoffer • bruce hogge • Ethan Holland • claire hollenbeck • William J. Holliman • Anthony Hollingworth • Ronald L. Hollis • Devin Holloway • stephen holmberg • Arryl Holmes • Clive Holtham • Jim Holub • Lior Homen • Ken Honeycutt • Jacky Hood • Kathryn Hood • Linda Hoopes • Anne Hopkins • Keith Hopper • Robert Horan • Andrew Horberry • Andrew Horesh • David Hornik • Robert Hornsby • David Horowitz • Michael Horsch Fizz • Mark Horsley • Brent Horst • Nemat Hossieny • Michael Hostetler • Douglas Hough • Jeff Howard • Carolyn Howard-Johnson • katy howell • Charles Howlett • Terry Hrynyshyn • Aliku Hsiao • cynthia hsieh • peihua hsieh • Alina Hsu • Christine Hsu • Francis Hsu • Jeffrey Hsu • Ricky Hsu • jeffrey hu • Xingcheng Hua • Bruce Huang • Daniel Huang • David Huang • Stan Huang • Zeke Huang • Jackie Huba • Don Huesman • Karen Huffman • Hugh Hughes • Michael Hughes • Sharon Hughes • erwan huhardeaux • H. S. Huhta • Niels Hundahl • Joseph Hunkins • Chuck Hunt • Alivia Hunter • Steven Hunter • Phil Hupfer • Pam Hurley • Tim Hutchinson • Rebeca Eun Young Hwang • Renae Hwang • Seong Yong Hwang • Youngmin Hwang • Christopher Iannuccilli • Mamane IBRAHIM • Masiar Ighani • NDUBUISI RICHARD IKEDIASHI • Nazeeruddin Ikram • ferhat ilhan • ron immink • Peter Indelicato • CBR India • George Infante • Lawrence Ingalls • Steve Ingersoll • John Inglis • Mathew Ingram • Bradley Inman • Motoko Inoue • Coyote inquiet • Viorel Iordache • ion iovu • adrian ipkins • Iñigo Irizar Arcelus • Eitan Iron • Gayle Irvin • Jim Isaak • Peter Isackson • Shinobu Ishizuka • Shariful Islam • John Isley • Greg Iszler • Julen Iturbe-Ormaetxe • Dmitri Ivanov • Dmitri Ivanov • Bill Ives • Carl Ivey • Ming Ivory • Manu Iyer • Prabhu Iyer • sunil iyer • Jacques Izard • jeff jack • Peter Wakefield Jackson • Toby Jackson • Bart Jacob • Bruno Jacob • Mathew Jacob • Dr Jack Jacoby • Martin Jaehn • Adil Jafry • Mohit Jaggi • Kenny Jahng • Amit Jain • Ashley Jain • Komal Jain • Sachin Jain • Sandeep Jain • Vaibhav jain • YOGESH JAIN • devebndra jaiswal • Nurzalina Jamaluddin • Dustin James • Joseph James • Sami Jan • William Jankel • Rene Jansen • Jan-Willem Janssen • Jean-Christophe Jardinier • Leslie Jarmon • Stephanie Jarrell • Saleem Javaid • Hoda Jawad • James Jaworowicz • Dinakar Jayarajan • Bhaskar Jayaraman • bryon jc • Kathleen Jefferis • joe jeffries • Brian Jelley • Debs Jenkins • Leighton Jenkins • Jon Jennett • Judy Jennings • David Jensen • Jeffrey Jensen • Paul Jensen • Avinash Jhangiani • ALMA RITA JIMENEZ • Hector Jose Jimenez Vargas • vivek jindgar • Praew Jitjuajun • kjefn jkhjk • Kal Joffres • T Johanix • earl johannaber • Brijesh John • Robert Johnsen • andrew Johnson • Arik Johnson • Bennett J. Johnson • Denise Johnson • Donald Johnson • Garold Johnson • Geoff Johnson • Jennifer Johnson • John Marshall Johnson • Jonathan Johnson • Katrina Johnson • Larry Johnson • Mark Johnson • Mike Johnson • Richard Johnson • Tim Johnson • david jhave johnston • Ken Johnston • Vinay Jokare • Hylton Jolliffe • Anne Jones • Bobby Jones • David Jones • DeDe Jones • Gary Jones • Janet Jones • Jason Jones • Kim Jones • Mary Jones • Michael Jones • Pepper Jones • Russell Jones • Stewart Jones • Tim Jones • Kristin Jordan • Paul Jorion • Andrew Joscelyne • Gustaf Josefsson • Georgia Joseph • Rodlyn Joseph • Amol Joshi • Mil Joshi • Neil Joshi • Tejas Joshi • Parimal Joshipura • Jay Joslin • jeremi joslin • Alain Jourdier • Hadi Jouyandeh • Alana Joyce • Alexandre Joyce • Steve Joyce • Susan Joyce • YF Juan • manuel julio • Marco Aurelio Julio • Nitin Julka • Shravan Jumani • INHWAN JUNG • Yvette Justice • shaji k • Houeida K. Anouar • Sachin Kadam • Dominic Kaeslin • Sam Kafando • rutger kahn • Michal Kainan-Koren • Bill Kaiser • Wes Kalbfleisch • Mohammed Kaleemuddin • Russell Kallman • s kalyanaraman • Sandeep Kamath • Subrahmanyam (Subbu) Kambhampati • David Kamien • Amar Kanade • Chipupu Kandeke • Bob Kane • Darilyn Kane • Gerald Kane • Marie Kane • mark kane • Dohyoung Kang • Hyun Ook Kang • Parm Kang • Richard Kang • Ramu Kannappan • Shashi Kant • ilteris kaplan • Michael Kaplan • Peter Kaplan • Ajit Kapoor • Amit Kapur • Kishore Karani • Tamilarasan Karapiah • Anand Karasi • Michelle Karczeski • Brian Kardon • ILGAR KARIMOV • benedict kariuki • Joakim Karlsson • Raman Karol • Kenneth Karpay • Tony Karrer • Eric Karsten • Hendrawan Kartika • Rajeev Karwal • Abdul Kasim • Stavros Katsios • Heidi Katz • Karen Katz • Keith Katz • Eric Kaufmann • gwen kautz • Katherine Kawamoto • Noritaka Kawashima • David Kay • Gareth Kay • Bob Kazmarowski • Sara Keating • Akshat Kedia • Heather Keegan • mike keesey • Karen Keeter • Joseph Kehoe • Thomas Kehoe • John Kellden • Thomas Kellerman • Patrick Gage Kelley • Rick Kelley • Chris Kelly • lois kelly • Michael Kelly • Molly Kelly • Eckhard Kemmerer • Tom Kendrick • Nimesh Kenia • David Kennan • Byron Kennedy • Dion Kenney • Robert Kenny • Rafael Kenski • Gabriel Kent • Mike Kenworthy • sultan kermally • Julien kervella • Cecelia Kessler • Steve Key • Tracey Keys • stephanie keyser • Craig Keyworth • Vinayak Khadye • Shagufta Khalil • Riaz Khan • Zaheer Khan • Vyom Khandelia • Nitin Khanna • Dipankar Khasnabish • Sandy Khaund • Mehnaz Khebar • Nader KHedr • Boris Khodorkovsky • Paul Kidder • Allene Kieff • Rick Kiley • Vida Killian • Esko Kilpi • Tuomas Kilpi • abe kim • David Kim • Hyun Jong Kim • Jae Yeon KIM • Min Kim • Sang Kim • YaeRi Kim • younju kim • JEFFREY KIMBALL • William Kimberly • Kevin Kimiak • Colleen Kindelin • Mary Lee Kingsley • Matthew Kinney • Carol J Kirk • David Kirkpatrick • Aron Kirschner • alex kirtland • Joel Kirvijn • Susan Kish • Stephen Kiwanuka-Kunsa • kjh kjh • Harry Klein • SJ Klein • Ira Kleinberg • art kleiner • Torben Klitgaard • Andrew Kluth • Dennis Kmiec • Anthony Knap • James Knapp • Jeff Knieriem • Jerry Knoll • Jayne Knoop • Christian Knothe • Susan Knowles • Cris Kobryn • Bujar Kocani • Brad Koch • Vivekanand Kochikar • Viswanathan Kodaganallur • KM Koenen • Walter Koepsell • David Kofol • gamba kohavi • Gregory Kohs • Aavo Kokk • Leonard Kolada • Craig Kolberg • Kazumi Komine • Kashyap Kompella • Miyuki Komuro • Deng Kong Meng • Paul Konnersman • Dave Konopka • maarten koomans • Luda Kopeikina • Heiner Koppermann • Yaron Koren • Christian Korff • Antti Korhonen • diana kornbrot • Nancy Korpela • pete kosa • Vadim Kosachev • Paul Kosempel • mathew koshy • Joseph Koskey • Tiffany Kosolcharoen • Vlatko Kotevski • Pradeep Koti Thathachari • Saroj Koul • George Kouleris • Terri Kowalchuk • Kevin koym • Derek Kozel • Bonnie Krabbenhoft • Ed Krajcir • Mark Krajewski • David Kram • Steve Krattiger • Jeffrey Krause • Greg Krauska • Rosa Krausz • Scott Krauthamer • Ana Kreacic-Lekovic • Kevin Kreitman • Kathryn Krenn • Matthew Krieger • Ashok Krish • Abinesh Krishan • anand krishnamoorthy • shankar krishnan • Vijaya krishnan • Jesper Krogstrup • patrick Kroner • David Kronfeld •

WE
ARE SMARTER THAN
ME

In a time where community and social networks are starting to infiltrate every aspect of our personal and professional lives, WE decided to test the notion that a book of business best practices could be written by "the crowd," and we are excited to have participated in this groundbreaking experiment.

As members of numerous communities ourselves: faculty, students, publishers and business people, WE—Wharton, Pearson, and MIT—believe that the outcome of this book is far better than anything WE as individuals could have authored in that it represents the collective wisdom of our respective communities, and a large number of individuals who joined the community during the course of the project. In the end, the physical book was authored in the conventional way (more about this in the Foreword), but it would not have been possible without the ongoing involvement and guidance from our communities.

Please join our commitment to WE by blogging, podcasting, discussing and writing your chapters, reviewing the ones we have created and posting reviews on the http://wearesmarter.org community website!

WE

ARE SMARTER THAN

ME

HOW TO UNLEASH THE POWER OF
CROWDS IN YOUR BUSINESS

BARRY LIBERT & JON SPECTOR
AND THOUSANDS OF CONTRIBUTORS

Vice President, Publisher: Tim Moore
Associate Editor-in-Chief and Director of Marketing: Amy Neidlinger
Wharton Editor: Yoram (Jerry) Wind
Editorial Assistant: Pamela Boland
Development Editor: Russ Hall
Digital Marketing Manager: Julie Phifer
Publicist: Amy Fandrei
Marketing Coordinator: Megan Colvin
Cover Designer: Ingredient
Managing Editor: Gina Kanouse
Senior Project Editor: Kristy Hart
Copy Editor: Krista Hansing Editorial Services, Inc.
Proofreader: Williams Woods Publishing
Senior Indexer: Cheryl Lenser
Interior Designer: Ingredient
Compositor: Jake McFarland
Manufacturing Buyer: Dan Uhrig

⊔⊔ Wharton School Publishing

Wharton School Publishing offers excellent discounts on this book when ordered in quantity for bulk purchases or special sales. For more information, please contact U.S. Corporate and Government Sales, 1-800-382-3419, corpsales@pearsontechgroup. com. For sales outside the U.S., please contact International Sales at international@ pearsoned.com.

Printed in the United States of America
First Printing September 2007
ISBN-10 0-13-224479-9
ISBN-13 978-0-13-224479-4

Pearson Education LTD.
Pearson Education Australia PTY, Limited.
Pearson Education Singapore, Pte. Ltd.
Pearson Education North Asia, Ltd.
Pearson Education Canada, Ltd.
Pearson Educatión de Mexico, S.A. de C.V.
Pearson Education—Japan
Pearson Education Malaysia, Pte. Ltd.

Library of Congress Cataloging-in-Publication Data
Libert, Barry.
  We are smarter than me : how to unleash the power of crowds in your business / Barry Libert, Jon Spector.
     p. cm.
  ISBN 0-13-224479-9 (hardback : alk. paper) 1. Strategic alliances (Business) 2. Social participation--Economic aspects. 3. Customer relations. 4. Customer services. 5. Marketing research. I. Spector, Jon, 1956- II. Title.
  HD69.S8.L53 2008
  658'.044--dc22
                              2007024024

Contents

Foreword—Social Networking Works

by Don Tapscott

Many people emphasize the *social* aspect of social networking. MySpace is growing at 2 million new registrants per week and with over 200 million members, is well on its way to half a billion. Most college students in the United States are on Facebook. There is a new blog created every second of every day. Over a million avatars live in a virtual community called Second Life.

But the smartest leaders see that the profitable word to emphasize when it comes to social networking is *working*. Deep down, nothing less than a new mode of production is in the making.

After all, if you can make an encyclopedia (Wikipedia) via social networking and mass collaboration, what else could you do? How about an operating system (Linux) or applications software (Sugar CRM is one of 125,000 open source applications projects underway)? How about a mutual fund (marketocracy.com), a peer-to-peer lending system (zopa.com), or designer T-shirts (threadless.com)? How about producing a television ad for the Super Bowl? Viewers of this year's Super Bowl XLI watched a Doritos advertisement that was created and chosen by its customers on the Internet. Perhaps a complex physical good like a motorcycle? The Chinese motorcycle industry—now the largest in the world—is a sprawling network of parts makers with no single company like Harley Davidson pulling the strings. Or take one of the world's the most complicated products—a new generation jumbo jet. Rather than painstakingly designing its supply chain, Boeing coinnovated the 787 Dreamliner with thousands of partners around the world in a mind-boggling peer-oriented ecosystem.

In this new world of collaboration, peers often come together to create value, often outside the walls of traditional companies. Consumer goods giant Procter & Gamble is a perfect example. Until recently, P&G was notoriously secretive, and it was failing, punctuated by a stock collapse in 2000. New CEO A. G. Lafley led the company on an ambitious campaign to restore P&G's greatness by sourcing 50 percent of its innovations from outside the company. Today, P&G searches for innovations in Web-enabled marketplaces such as InnoCentive, NineSigma, and yet2.com. These so-called eBays for innovation have led to hundreds of new products, some of which turned out to be home runs. Five years after the stock implosion, P&G has doubled its share price and now boasts a portfolio of 22 billion-dollar brands.

Around the same time, gold-mining company Goldcorp was in a similar pickle. Its geologists could not determine whether its ailing mines held any more ore. The corporation was on the brink of folding. CEO Rob McEwan did something unheard of in his industry. He published all of the company's previously secret geological data on the Web and held a contest to so see if anyone could help find gold on the property. Seventy-seven submissions came from around the world, some using techniques and technologies Goldcorp had not heard of. For $500,000 in prizes, Goldcorp found over $3 billion of gold and the company's market value multiplied several times over. By opening up and collaborating, Goldcorp's shareholders prospered.

Predictably however, revolutionary new modes of production bring dislocation and confusion. They are often received with coolness or worse—outright mockery or hostility. Vested interests fight against change. Leaders of the old have great difficulty embracing the new. Others are concerned that the incentives for knowledge producers are disappearing in a world where individuals can pool their talents to create free goods that compete with proprietary marketplace offerings. People as wise as Bill Gates have argued that capitalism is undermined by any movement to assemble a global "creative commons" that contains large bodies of scientific and cultural content. They fear that these massive communities and new business models will reduce the proportion of our economy available for profitable activity.

The examples in this book suggest otherwise. With more than a billion individuals around the world connected by a new multimedia high-bandwidth medium of human communications, collaboration and teamwork have become the business world's biggest drivers of success. Companies are eclipsing competitors by linking with suppliers and customers to share information, innovate, and execute. By harnessing the wisdom and ability of individuals and crowds, both inside and outside their boundaries, smart companies in every industry are thriving.

This is likely the first book you have read, created in collaboration with a crowd, and as such, I hope you will remember it and find it useful. But it won't be your last. My hope is that it may inspire you to get involved in the mass collaboration revolution and, in doing so, engage with others, have fun, and prosper.

>   **Don Tapscott,** Chief Executive of the think tank
>   New Paradigm and the author of 11 books, most
>   recently, with Anthony D. Williams, *Wikinomics:
>   How Mass Collaboration Changes Everything*

Authors' Note—How We Got Here

Five years ago, when we first had the experience that led to this book, the notion that a group might be smarter than any of its members was a complete non-starter. By definition, groupthink was the lowest common denominator; everyone knew that a camel was a horse designed by a committee. Today, thanks to a clutch of best-selling books, we know better. But even now, although crowdsourcing, wikinomics, and open-source technology have become buzzwords in the business world, there is no practical guide to translate those concepts into usable tools and techniques. This book fills that gap, describing in detail how businesses of all kinds can make the wisdom of crowds work for them. It's intended for all those businesspeople who want to tap into the power and talent of the online masses and are wondering how to go about it.

We stumbled on the basic idea as colleagues in a rapidly growing startup. One of the companies we acquired specialized in call-center management. The company had assembled a group of 200 executives, each of them running one or more call centers. These people actively collaborated with each other and collectively knew more about call centers than just about anyone. So when one of them was faced with a technical or strategic problem, he or she could turn to the other members of the group for advice, and count on getting it. In effect, rather than functioning simply as individual managers who turned to consultants for assistance, the members had learned to work as a community, and consistently offered each other collective advice that no single person or consultant could possibly provide.

For Barry, that story triggered the insight that led to this book. His idea was that companies of every kind could profitably and cost-effectively make the most of the knowledge and resources held by communities of like-minded people, whether they were employees, customers, partners, or investors. He went on to expand the call-center business into a company dedicated to helping other organizations tap the power of community. He called it Shared Insights.

Barry decided that a book was needed to share his rapidly growing experience and knowledge with a wider audience. But true to the basic concept, he didn't want to write it himself. It should be produced by a community, whose collectively shared ideas and insights would inevitably be better than any single author's.

Meanwhile, Jon was embarking on a new career as an educator. In 2004, he was named vice dean and director of executive education at The Wharton School of the University of Pennsylvania. A few months later, he learned Barry was looking for a partner to build the community that would write this book. Soon Jon signed onto the project.

The timing was serendipitous. James Surowiecki's *The Wisdom of Crowds*, which suggested that the masses have an intelligence that exceeds that of traditional experts, was a best seller. An even more widely read book, *Wikinomics: How Mass Collaboration Changes Everything*, by Don Tapscott and Anthony D. Williams, was to follow, showing how some companies are using mass collaboration and open-source technology to beat the competition. Wikipedia, the online encyclopedia whose content is produced by its readers, had become an Internet staple. Thomas Friedman's *The World Is Flat* would suggest that not only are crowds smart, they are highly connected and can do wondrous things. The irony was that hardly anyone except Wikipedia was actually mobilizing collective writing—as Surowiecki himself noted dryly, "I alone wrote this book." Our book would be the first of its kind, a breakthrough project. And Jon knew just the right publisher for a book written by a community.

The year before, Wharton had reached an agreement with Pearson Education to create and distribute business books. The two organizations were intrigued by Barry's proposal, and thus we began to hammer out an agreement with Wharton and Pearson as our publishers and supporters of the proposed book-writing community.

That's when some hard questions surfaced. With a community of hundreds or potentially thousands of people taking part in the writing, who would get what share of the royalties? Who would own the intellectual property? How would decisions be made about which chapters to include and what text to select?

We finally set up www.wearesmarter.org in the fall of 2006. It explained our goal, and nearly 3,000 people responded almost immediately. They had all sorts of ideas about how communities could help businesses and how the book could be put together. They also requested, appropriately, that we support the new community with a full cadre of moderators. Our project was, for a time, overwhelmed as bloggers, podcasters, potential authors, and would-be editors joined the community. Many also attended the first Community 2.0 event in Las Vegas. In the end, we found the actual text of the book, the flow of the topics, and the graphical design had to be produced in the conventional way, rather than relying on the crowd to perform these functions. But it is fair to say that what you are reading is a combination of our community's insights from all these activities and our own research. And the callout quotes you will find scattered throughout the book are drawn directly from our members' wikis, podcasts, discussion posts, and in-person comments from the Community 2.0 event.

The hard questions got solved. The community agreed that the royalties would go to charity, and every person who contributed to the project will have an equal voice in selecting which charities will get the money.

Furthermore, the online community is still very much alive. As of spring 2007, there were 4,375 members, 737 discussion forum posts, and more than 250 wiki contributors generating 1,600 wiki posts. And we are planning another book in which even more of the community's case studies and contributions will be included.

In hindsight, the story of our community-driven odyssey is an exciting tale, with ups and downs that are not all that uncommon when ground-breaking initiatives are attempted. As we point out in the pages ahead, many companies have benefited hugely from harnessing collective power. But not all have succeeded. As we will also detail, there are many pitfalls to be avoided and obstacles to be overcome in tapping the wisdom of communities.

If you are willing to take on the challenge, you have a good chance of being handsomely rewarded. Communities can help companies—your company—invent new products and services, improve customer service, boost sales, turbo-charge manufacturing, tap into new sources of financing, and make everyone a leader. They can make your company more productive, more profitable, and a better place for the people who work and live there.

This book tells you how to make that happen. Let's get started.

01

Look What We Can Do

At the ripe old age of 15, the Web has already changed
human society so profoundly that historians have begun
comparing the Internet Age with the Renaissance and the
Industrial Revolution. The Web has connected nearly a billion
people. With that many brains as its motivating force, the
transformation forged by the Internet
has morphed from quantitative to
qualitative: The power of the collective
"we" is nearly unfathomable. Each
of those brains has some 10 billion
neurons linked to one another
through about 10,000 synapses. Now
all that individual brainpower is tied
together and amplified by the power of
technology: The new and potent "we" is
far smarter than any singular "me." For
the first time, humans can act in mass collaboration, using
the kind of collective intelligence once reserved for ants and
bees—but now with human IQ driving the mix. The result is
a quantum increase in the world's ability to conceive, create,
compute, and connect. We are only beginning to comprehend
the consequences.

"If at first the idea is not absurd,
there is no hope for it."

—ALBERT EINSTEIN

Cyberwatchers say the Internet has evolved in two distinct stages: Web 1.0 and Web 2.0. In both of them, the Net has been a hugely fertile market where people turn data into money. But Web 1.0 winners profited (mainly in the dot-com boom) by cornering data for themselves and riding the price up. Web 2.0 innovators do the opposite. They believe information becomes more valuable as more people use it. Instead of  tightly controlling the code behind a new software program, for example, they let anyone alter or add to it, confident that the users will contribute their own ideas and improve the program for everyone. The miracle is that, by giving away access, the owners can actually reduce their own costs while winding up with a better product, certified as such by its volunteer creators—a product that can win ever more customers.

As a business model, that process is called open sourcing or *crowdsourcing*—it turns over tasks traditionally performed by employees to the Internet multitude. And it has claimed some memorable successes, particularly on the product-development front. Mozilla's Firefox open-source Web browser, for example, has been downloaded more than 300 million times and is used by an estimated 70 million to 80 million people. The Linux operating system, created as an open-source alternative to Windows and UNIX, can be downloaded free and altered to suit any user's needs; with all that firepower brought to bear, bugs in the system get fixed in a matter of hours. Some five million users per month swear by Wikipedia, the free online encyclopedia created and updated by Internet volunteers to the tune of two million articles and counting. Any visitor can edit *most* of its articles, although some, such as the entry on George W. Bush, are protected by volunteer administrators. That's because ideologues and mischief-makers occasionally take liberties with the facts, but the process is self-correcting as other users and administrators set them straight.

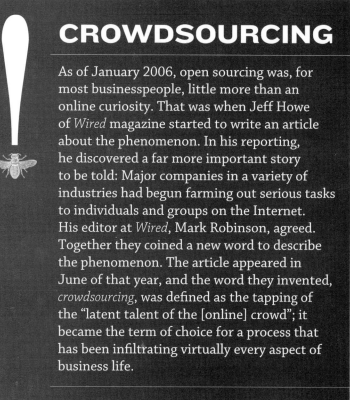

CROWDSOURCING

As of January 2006, open sourcing was, for most businesspeople, little more than an online curiosity. That was when Jeff Howe of *Wired* magazine started to write an article about the phenomenon. In his reporting, he discovered a far more important story to be told: Major companies in a variety of industries had begun farming out serious tasks to individuals and groups on the Internet. His editor at *Wired*, Mark Robinson, agreed. Together they coined a new word to describe the phenomenon. The article appeared in June of that year, and the word they invented, *crowdsourcing*, was defined as the tapping of the "latent talent of the [online] crowd"; it became the term of choice for a process that has been infiltrating virtually every aspect of business life.

Savvy companies are turning to the Internet hordes for help with new product development, customer service, sales, production, finance, and even management. They prosper by searching out, nurturing, and tapping the expertise of individual online communities, customers included.

The actual numbers of companies using online mass collaboration are surprising. Early in 2007, Forrester Research reported that a survey of 119 chief intelligence officers found that fully 89 percent were using at least one of six technologies for collective intelligence, including such unlikely business tools as podcasts, wikis, blogs, and social networking. A worldwide McKinsey & Company survey of 2,800 ranking executives found that the leading country in the trend was India, with 80 percent of its companies planning to increase their spending for online communities over the next three years. North America, with 65 percent planning increases, came in third, just behind companies in the Asia-Pacific region.

Naturally, there are pitfalls in crowdsourcing. If collaboration isn't done right, it had best not be done at all. Gartner Research has predicted, with 80 percent certainty, that by 2010, more than 60 percent of *Fortune* 1,000 companies will have some form of online community that can be used in marketing—but with the same degree of confidence, Gartner says half of those will be so poorly managed that they will do more harm than good.

"We're Going to Aggressively Expose Ourselves!"

Long before there was an Internet, of course, the power of mass collaboration was evident. From the hive of the honey bee to the barn-raisings of rural America, many communities have relied upon intense and all-but-universal cooperation. In the case of the honey bee, a system of signals, ranging from the release of a particular scent to the dance of a forager, triggers the crowd actions that keep the hive buzzing. Barn-raisings are inspired by a more conscious recognition of the benefits of mutual dependence.

Jeff Bezos, founder, chairman, and chief executive officer of Amazon.com, was thinking more about the benefits of a loyal customer base when he established Amazon's online customer reviews, which might have been the first clear example of business crowdsourcing. Done for no pay and with no controls by the company, they added real value to Amazon's offerings. They also inspired Bezos to take his business in a radical new direction.

During its first decade, the company had invested more than $2 billion to build and safeguard its giant database of proprietary information, including pricing, sales, customers, book reviews, and inventory data. In 2004, Bezos asked his senior management team a radical question: What if they opened the vault to public scrutiny so everyone could use the database?

Ever the contrarian, he advocated sharing Amazon's knowledge as a way of profiting even more from it. By letting savvy outsiders in, he argued, Amazon would enter into potentially profitable partnerships with them. Not all his colleagues were enthusiastic about the idea, but, in the end, Bezos prevailed. He ended the debate by opening his arms wide and declaring, "We're going to aggressively expose ourselves!"

The impact has been nothing short of phenomenal. Since Bezos made his bold move, more than 240,000 people have participated in what is now known as Amazon Web Services, and the number of software developers and entrepreneurs clamoring to join the crowd continues to grow at a rapid clip, up by more than 55 percent in the 12 months through January 2007. No longer a risky experiment, crowdsourcing is now a core part of Amazon's strategy. Collectively, the programmers and businesses that scurried to get a look at what Amazon knew have greatly expanded its knowledge and field of operations, developing hundreds of new shopping interfaces that have drawn millions of customers and vastly increased the company's sales and profits.

Independent entrepreneurs such as Daryl Butcher, Jason Meyer, and Hector Rivas, for instance, have sold millions of dollars' worth of used books since linking up with Amazon. Volume is the main strategic focus of their online Thrift Books venture—of necessity: How else could a company survive, let alone prosper, by selling books for as little as a penny? Instead of being bogged down in the time-wasting,

money-losing tedium of cataloguing books by hand, Thrift
Books has relied on Amazon's efficient technology to become
one of the largest used-book sellers in the country, with
revenues of more than $2.5 million a year.

Other innovative ideas also can find a welcoming and
profitable home on Amazon. More than one million
merchants, potential customers, showcase their wares,
both new and used, on the site. ScoutPal, a technology
that enables a cell phone or other wireless device to
read bar codes, was one of those ideas that took
flight after linking up with Amazon. It was born
from one woman's problems in selling used books
on the site.

Barbara Anderson shopped at yard and tag sales, but often
found she paid more than she should have and couldn't
recoup her investment, much less earn a profit. Her husband,
Dave, experienced at writing software for wireless gadgets,
stepped in to help. The program he came up with allowed
Barbara to access Amazon's Web Services database using her
cell phone. She could enter a book's bar code and instantly
learn the price any given title was fetching on Amazon
and how many copies were available for sale. With that
information in hand,
she was able to buy
only those books
she could profitably
resell. The result: Her
income rose threefold
to $100,000, of which
some 85 percent was
profit. And there was a
bonus: Her husband's

ScoutPal application has become a second Amazon-based family business, with more than 1,000 subscribers, each paying $10 a month.

Jeff Bezos has found yet another role for Amazon's huge community: In 2005, Bezos created a Web site to enroll volunteers in the task of finding duplicates among the millions of Amazon Web pages—a task that his software could not handle. The volunteers were given a few cents for each duplicate page they found. The process worked well, so Bezos turned it into a business. The Web site was renamed Mturk.com, and Amazon invited software developers to tap into it for such tasks as finding specific objects in photos, translating text, and judging the beauty of a scene or object.

The name of the service, Amazon Mechanical Turk, is a tongue-in-cheek homage to an eighteenth-century hoax in which a life-size mannequin, attired in a turban and robe, was able to take on all comers—and defeat most of them—in well-publicized chess matches. As was eventually discovered, a human chess master was hidden inside the "Mechanical Turk" machine.

Amazon has more than 100,000 so-called Turk workers today, in more than 100 countries. They are paid only pennies for their HITs (human intelligence tasks), and Bezos has been criticized for running a virtual sweatshop.

But the workers seem willing enough. Some see it as a kind of hobby, or a virtual jigsaw puzzle. One disabled veteran told a reporter that he could earn about $100 a week by working two hours a day for the Turk, and he called it "a form of therapy to get [him] used to working again."

The Turk's customers are satisfied, too. iConclude, a software company that sells automated programs to troubleshoot and repair information technology networks, posted a request on Mturk.com for one simple procedure and got replies from 300 programmers. Sunny Gupta, iConclude's CEO, says he got the job done for one-tenth what it would have cost in his own shop—and after the volunteers were paid, the Turk's fee was just an additional 10 percent.

A WORD FROM WE

"What becomes clear is that companies need knowledge that is accessible only via their employees and their customers and their advisors. It suddenly matters how we relate to other people in the organization, who knows who, and the nature of their relationship."

—CHAPTER 1, "THE ORIGINS OF COMMUNITY" SECTION, AT WWW.WEARESMARTER.ORG

Amazon, of course, was just one of the pioneers in the crowdsourcing field. From the Internet telephone upstart Skype to eBay's massive auctions, new business models have sprung from online collaboration, and traditional companies such as Procter & Gamble, Hewlett-Packard, LEGO, and Eli Lilly are using communities in marketing, product development, customer relations, and even basic research and design. As some see it, the concentration of economic power that began in the Industrial Revolution is actually being reversed. University of Michigan business professor C. K. Prahalad has called the wikinomics trend "the democratization of industry," foreshadowing nothing less than "an economy of the people, by the people, and for the people."

Canada's Cambrian House entered the crowdsourcing lists in 2006 with a business premise that was simplicity itself: The best way to uncover new ideas for software and then pick the winners is to rely on software users themselves. That made for a somewhat startling offer when Cambrian's founder, Michael Sikorsky, was pitching the idea to his first investors. "We don't know what we're going to build, who will build it, or who will buy what we make," he said. He raised $2.6 million anyway, and the pot has since grown to more than $8 million.

Sikorsky's model has worked so well that Cambrian House now has fully 30,000 community members dreaming up ideas, trying them out, collaborating on improvements, compensating each other for their time and work, and buying the final product. Those offerings have since grown beyond software to include entirely new businesses and even some physical goods. The company's guiding question (and answer): "How would you unleash the ideas, talents, and entrepreneurial drive of six billion people? Bring them together under one roof."

Here's how Cambrian House's crowdsourcing model works today.

A member of Cambrian's community—a student, an entrepreneur, a business advisor, an investor, a designer, or a game player—submits an idea. The community members rank it according to marketability and ease of distribution over the Internet. The feedback from the community helps the person who submitted the idea refine his or her concept and determine whether it merits becoming a commercial reality.

Cambrian House also helps highlight the community's hottest ideas in a tournament called IdeaWarz. Sixteen ideas compete head to head in four elimination rounds. Each week, the community votes to eliminate half of the IdeaWarz

contestants until a single champion is left. The winning proposal garners funding and fame. The contest is, in many ways, a filtering tool using the wisdom of crowds to determine the best idea in the community at that moment.

It also gives those who submit ideas the validation they need to feel confident that time and resources can now be dedicated to turning an idea into a business with the community's help.

They then connect with community members to write code for the program, develop a business plan, design a logo, and so on in exchange for royalty points or Cambros (Cambrian House's internal currency: One Cambros equals $1). Royalty points ensure a contributor shares in the product's profitability.

The Cambrian development community of programmers, graphic designers, copywriters, illustrators, and the like bring the concept to life. If it flops, well, better luck next time. If it takes off, the inventor and the members they worked with reap the rewards. As the builders of the platform responsible for helping its members connect and bring ideas to life, Cambrian House allows all those who submit ideas to maintain ownership of their intellectual property, but it plans to earn revenue by implementing minor transaction fees at some point (when royalties and Cambros are exchanged between members), and does invest in some ideas.

Determined to work with their community as partners, Cambrian House shares 1 percent of its annual profits with its community (a member co-op board determines how the funds are allocated).

To date, Cambrian House
has invested in four
crowdsourced products

that have come to the market. The first to produce revenues
was Prezzle.com, which enables you to send a friend online
greetings and gift certificates from vendors such as Amazon,
Bath & Body Works, and Sephora. You can choose your
wrapping paper, provide clues to what the gift is, and pick
the date it can be opened. Prezzle's revenues are modest—a
projected $1 million for 2008—but CEO Sikorsky hopes some
viral marketing and savvy business development partnership
will enable Prezzle to reach its tipping point.

Another of Cambrian's ventures, a desktop-to-desktop
combat game called Gwabs, started off as a big hit in
community forums, prompting the company to invest $8,000
in a market test. After selling hundreds of the games over
just one weekend, Cambrian poured another $100,000 into
developing the product for retail sale. All told, the company
spent only six months and $200,000 to turn the idea into a
marketable product, Sikorsky says, less than half the time and
a third of the cost of developing it in-house.

By harnessing the power of crowds, more businesspeople
can make—and are making—better decisions and bigger
profits. In mid-2006, for example, IBM invited its entire
community—employees, their family members, and
customers—to take part in a brainstorming session to
identify potential areas for innovation. In the first session
of the "innovation jam," fully 150,000 online volunteers
were given 72 hours to come up with ideas. They produced
46,000 suggestions, which the company's staffers sifted and
evaluated; then, in September, the online conclave assembled
again to vote on the ideas with the most potential.

BY HARNESSING THE POWER OF CROWDS, MORE BUSINESSPEOPLE CAN MAKE—AND ARE MAKING— BETTER DECISIONS AND BIGGER PROFITS.

A WORD FROM WE

"If you're engaging your community online, you have the ability to create that trust and then that loyalty, which has to be mutual."

—CRAIG NEWMARK, FOUNDER OF CRAIGSLIST

IBM's CEO, Sam Palmisano, has promised to put as much as $100 million into developing the 10 winning ideas—and he will have a hand in the final choice.

The e.Lilly division of pharmaceutical giant Eli Lilly was among the first to harness the collaborative power of the Internet when in 2001 it launched Innocentive, the first online, incentive-based scientific network created specifically for the global research and development community. Innocentive's online platform allowed world-class scientists and R&D-based companies to collaborate to achieve innovative solutions to complex challenges. Innocentive offers "seeker companies" the opportunity to increase their R&D potential by posting challenges without violating their confidentiality and intellectual property interests. Seeker companies might be looking for a chemical to be used in art restoration, for instance, or the efficient synthesis of butane tetracarboxylic acid. David Bradin, a patent attorney from Seattle, was paid $4,000 for his tetracarboxylic acid formula. P&G says Innocentive has increased the share of its new products originating outside the company from 20 percent to 35 percent.

Though still in its infancy, crowdsourcing is already rewriting the rules of business, posing major challenges and opening up unprecedented opportunities. The chapters that follow address the specifics of the trend, from product development and marketing to production, financing, management techniques, and even strategy. Coming up:

❖ Chapter 2, "Go from R&D to R&WE," shows how to use communities to spot new market opportunities, identify benefits, and sharpen new products and services. Among the pioneering companies featured: Brewtopia, Idea Crossing, General Mills, Kraft, Linden Lab, and Procter & Gamble.

❖ Chapter 3, "How May We Help We?", shows how to make use of communities to improve service and increase customer satisfaction. Among the businesses featured: Bradbury Software, Cookshack, Intuit, and PMI Audio Group.

❖ Chapter 4, "Customer, Sell Thyself," provides insights into the use of community-based techniques to reduce selling and marketing costs while boosting customer loyalty. Cases in point: MasterCard, Nike, and the Portland Trailblazers.

❖ Chapter 5, "If We Build It, We Will Come," shares lessons about how communities are changing methods and best practices in factories, virtual and otherwise, around the world. Companies whose experiences are detailed include: iStockphoto, Reevoo, ThisNext, and Zebo.

❖ Chapter 6, "Welcome to the World Bank of We," explains how to tap communities to help fund business growth and support worthy charitable causes. Prosper is one of the primary examples cited.

❖ Chapter 7, "Make Everyone a C-We-O," sheds
   light on how to use communities to organize and
   manage companies. The centerpiece case study:
   TheBusinessExperiment.com.

❖ Chapter 8, "Lead from the Rear," details some of the key
   lessons we learned in the course of our experiment with
   wearesmarter.org.

We'll start at the beginning: What are you going to sell? Years
ago, the late, lamented Packard luxury car came up with a
classic slogan, "Ask the man who owns one." These days,
some of the country's leading corporations are doing just that,
asking their own customers for help in creating new products
and services and improving old ones. The chapter just ahead
explores that trend, describing the impressive results these
organizations are achieving and how they go about it—and
how you can, too.

02

Go from R&D to R&We

Back in the Aussie summer of 2002, Liam Mulhall was ready to abandon the high-stress, high-tech business. He had put in his time at the local office of Red Hat, the big U.S.-based provider of open sourcing solutions, and now he and his two buddies had a new Plan A. They wanted to buy a pub in Sydney. The problem was, the price was more than the lads could afford. So they fell back on Plan B, which, in this case, was Plan Brew. With a nothing-to-lose attitude—"It was our money and not a lot of it," Mulhall allows—they would make beer, but with a twist; they were going to tap the power of community.

Mulhall had stumbled onto the story of PK-35, a Finnish soccer club. The team's coach invited fans to determine its recruiting, training, and even game tactics by allowing them to vote using their cell phones. The idea put the fizz in Mulhall's lager. As he would later write, he had found "the best way to run a business—give the customers the reins."

"Innovation is simply group intelligence having fun."

—MICHAEL NOLAN

Luckily, Mulhall and his two friends didn't know that the 2002 soccer season would be so disastrous that PK-35 would fire its coach and scrap its fan-driven ways. So they went ahead with their scheme, setting up a Web site, Brewtopia. com.au, and inviting 140 of their friends to describe their ideal beer. Within weeks, the community had built up a head of more than 10,000 people in 20 countries, and their votes determined everything from the beer's style (lager), color (pale amber), and alcohol content (4.5 percent) to the shape of the bottle and the colors printed on the label.

The founders, however, were—and are—solely responsible for the beer's name. For reasons comprehensible only to an Australian (let's just say it has to do with sheep), they called it Blowfly.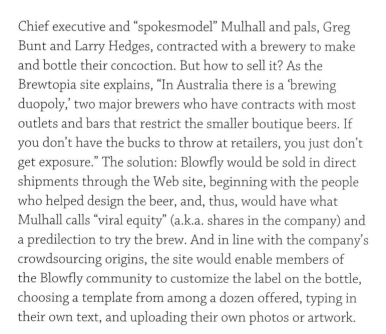

Chief executive and "spokesmodel" Mulhall and pals, Greg Bunt and Larry Hedges, contracted with a brewery to make and bottle their concoction. But how to sell it? As the Brewtopia site explains, "In Australia there is a 'brewing duopoly,' two major brewers who have contracts with most outlets and bars that restrict the smaller boutique beers. If you don't have the bucks to throw at retailers, you just don't get exposure." The solution: Blowfly would be sold in direct shipments through the Web site, beginning with the people who helped design the beer, and, thus, would have what Mulhall calls "viral equity" (a.k.a. shares in the company) and a predilection to try the brew. And in line with the company's crowdsourcing origins, the site would enable members of the Blowfly community to customize the label on the bottle, choosing a template from among a dozen offered, typing in their own text, and uploading their own photos or artwork.

Four years later, in 2007, with, as Mulhall would have it, "no brewing experience, no industry experience, no marketing

experience, no money, and no idea what [they] were doing,"
Brewtopia had 50,000 customers in 46 nations. Having
already branched out to wine and bottled water, soft drinks
were on the way, Mulhall told London-based marketing
consultant Johnnie Moore. Brewtopia also sells brand-
promoting T-shirts and caps.

Mulhall and his buddies give Brewtopia a wisecracking zest
that appeals to their young customers, further reinforcing
the sense of community. "Some people think this is a cheap
publicity stunt," the Web site proclaims. "Well, there's
nothing cheap about it!" If customers don't like the beer,
the message adds, "you're in desperate need of a taste bud
transplant—but we'd rather not foot the bill for that—
instead we'll gladly refund your money in return for the
unused beer as long as you give us your feedback on what
didn't 'work for you.'"

In his telephone interview with Moore, conducted, fittingly
enough, via Skype, Mulhall declared that a business has to
constantly keep moving, reinventing itself "like Madonna."
For Brewtopia, which is now flush with cash from its initial
public offering on Australia's National Stock Exchange, the
next move is into retail. "Unless you drop your stuff in a
shop, people don't believe you are a real company," he said.
As for Mulhall himself, he just might have a go at the financial
industry, specifically
community banking, where
giving customers a voice
in how the business is run
could be a differentiating
feature with great appeal
(more on this topic later in
the book).

The Community Is Always Right

For businesses large and small, in
Australia and elsewhere, it's no
inconsequential decision to let
customers dictate what is sold. New
product development is among
the most important activities
any enterprise undertakes. A

business lives or dies on the strength of what it offers, and it's
understandable that leaders often resist losing control over
the basic nature of the goods they sell.

But there's much to be said for tapping the collective wisdom
of a community—customer or otherwise—for product ideas
and improvements. In the case of customers, it gives them
a vested interest in the results and all but guarantees they
will like—and buy—what they've created. You might even be
able to skip the whole test-marketing process (but, of course,
that's up to you).

Imagine the computers that Acer or Gateway or Hewlett-
Packard could create with input from customers—
computers made not for geeks who love to install
memory cards and new software, but for
the rest of us, who like to drive cars
without having to know how to
repair the fuel injector.

In the pages that follow are a host of examples of innovative
organizations that, like Brewtopia, have pioneered product
development by people not on their payroll. These businesses
range from food giants to the inventors of a popular virtual
world that has confounded skeptics who believed only

nerds would sign on. These organizations' commitment to the collaborative process ranges from cautious to total immersion.

Nikoli

Maki Kaji likes to bet on the ponies, which explains why, when he started a puzzle magazine in 1980, he named it *Nikoli* in honor of a winning racehorse. The quarterly magazine, based in Tokyo, turned out to be a good bet, too. It offers some 30 different types of puzzles with each issue, and a third of them are brand new. They are the handiwork not of the company's employees, but of its readers.

Kaji is the world's most prolific pencil-and-paper puzzle creator, and he publishes them by the hundreds in *Nikoli* and in all sorts of books and other puzzle magazines. But he relies on others to do the creating. In the case of Sudoku, for example, which Kaji promoted around the globe, the inventor was an American. For the rest, he looks to his tens of thousands of subscribers.

They submit their ideas for new kinds of puzzles, a staff of 20 goes through them, and the most promising appear in the next issue of *Nikoli*. Readers then send in their reactions and critiques. Out of that process, Kaji has winnowed some 250 new kinds of puzzles, which get printed in his books.

In the case of Sudoku, he trademarked the game in Japan but nowhere else, so he receives no royalties from the huge sales of the game around the world. He claims to be unfazed, and he has no intention of trademarking other new games. "This openness is more in keeping with *Nikoli's* open culture," he told the *New York Times.* "We're prolific because we do it for the love of the games, not the money." He prides himself on never having advertised *Nikoli,* letting the Japanese love of mathematics and games do the selling.

Working a puzzle is like being at the track, he explains: "Not just the fun of solving it, but the excitement before, even if you don't solve it. It's that excitement before the finish line when the horses are roaring down the stretch and you're cheering them on."

Nikoli first published a complicated version of Sudoku in 1984. Its readers offered their modifications and corrections until Kaji had a puzzle he thought was a winner, and it caught on in Japan. But it wasn't until the *London Times* picked it up 20 years later that Sudoku took off. And that put Kaji and his company in the spotlight as puzzle promoters. Lately, another community-provided numbers puzzle from *Nikoli,* called Kakuro, has been taking the world by storm.

WHAT YOU CAN DO

* **The medium is not the message.**
Before the Internet and e-mail invaded our lives, Maki Kaji was tapping the talent of his magazine community by snail mail. A company's goal is to convince us, as the necessary "we," to take part; the means of communication, important though it be, is secondary.

* **Know your neighbors.** Because Kaji identified with his readers and understood them so well, he knew he could count on them to join the game-invention game.

Procter & Gamble

For generations, the research and development (R&D) team at Procter & Gamble, 9,000-strong, had been the stuff of business legend, cranking out dozens of high-profile, high-profit new products year after year. But in 2000, A. G. Lafley, the company's newly arrived chairman and chief executive officer, stunned his prideful researchers. They were not, he announced, producing winners

A WORD FROM WE

"One of the main reasons that people get involved as a community participant for a company is because of the pain they experience with the product or the service. In the pain-solving process, the company learns so much about how to make their products better."

—DENISE HOWELL, BLOGGER

big enough or fast enough to significantly boost corporate revenues. His solution was drastic: By the end of the decade, fully half of all new P&G products and technologies would have to come from outside the company.

The object, Lafley insisted, was not to supplant the mighty in-house R&D effort, but to supplement it. That turned out to be a vastly difficult venture, though, and no wonder, given the company's size and complexity. For one thing, the internal communication systems had to be reinvented to make it possible for all parts of the company to exchange data and brainstorm. Then that information had to be made available to noncompany entities, including suppliers and distributors.

Another stumbling block was the resistance of many of P&G's key researchers. Some complained that the proposed changes in their way of doing things would stifle creativity. Others feared a loss of power and prestige if their information and work had to be shared.

Lafley persevered. His most drastic move was a giant step into crowdsourcing. P&G put together a global community made up of high-tech entrepreneurs and open networks such as NineSigma, and including the retired scientists and engineers of YourEncore and the  marketplace for intellectual property exchange called Yet2. com. P&G has also gone to Innocentive, a network of 120,000 self-selected technical people from more than 175 countries who receive cash awards if their ideas prove out.

In seeking help from its extended community, P&G submits so-called "science problems" for solutions. Sometimes the problems come from in-house R&D, representing blind alleys those researchers have come up against. Sometimes the company asks its online partners for help in adapting a feature of a competitor's product to one of its own. The right answers have greatly benefited P&G. In the case of Innocentive, for example, a third of the dozens of problems posed have been solved. One crisp example of an early crowdsourcing triumph: When the company was stymied for a way to print messages on its Pringles potato chips, the development community found a bakery in Italy with a little-publicized process that could do the job.

P&G is closing in on Lafley's goal. As of 2006, the company was deriving 35 percent of its ideas from outsiders. Meanwhile, R&D productivity has soared 60 percent. A whopping 80 percent of its product launches are successful, compared to 30 percent for the consumer-products industry  as a whole. And it spends 3.1 percent, or about $2.1 billion, of its more than $68 billion in annual worldwide revenue on research and development, much more than others in the industry.

WHAT YOU CAN DO

- **Tread firmly but carefully.** Seeking the help of outsiders, even when they're part of some amorphous, unseen community, can be threatening to in-house staff. They will resist. Make your intentions clear, as P&G's Lafley did, and  stick to them. Meanwhile, do everything possible to accommodate the concerns of the resisters. For example, P&G allowed researchers to type up their notes in Microsoft Word or continue to rely on an older system that was modified to make it compatible with the new pilot technology.

- **Thank you for sharing.** Ironically, some of the same companies that have seen the crowdsourcing light and reached outside their walls have overlooked the wealth of intelligence and experience in the nontechnical side of their operations. The days of kissing off employees' ideas with a couple of suggestion boxes is long past. No business can afford  to ignore the ideas and inside knowledge brewing in the minds of its accountants and lawyers, production line, and sales crew, just waiting for management to provide an incentive to join in.

Linden Lab

General Motors has created a whole complex where you can
go to a drive-in theater or a tune-up shop and, oh yes, check
out the Pontiac Solstice. Dell has a factory where you can
customize your PC and have it shipped to your door. Reuters
has set up a newsroom to help you keep up with what's going
on in the world. And you can enjoy it all without moving an
inch from your office desk or your easy chair.

You're in Second Life, the online virtual universe. Some
people are still calling it a game, but they don't include GM,
Dell, Reuters, and dozens of other corporations. They see this
ultimate example of crowdsourcing as strictly business.

The handiwork of Linden Lab, a San Francisco–based 3D
entertainment company, Second Life has been and is being
shaped entirely by its five million or so members. They are
represented by cartoonlike avatars who can go to casinos, sex
clubs, and shopping malls; attend concerts (Suzanne Vega
and Duran Duran have performed there); design furniture;
invent weapons; and drive cars. They can also devise alternate
lifestyles, make new friends, start new careers, and adopt a
new personality.

Second Lifers can also get
their virtual flu shots from
a virtual employee of the Centers
for Disease Control and Prevention; bump into
House Speaker Nancy Pelosi and other political types
on Capitol Hill island; and attend college-level lectures
in virtual classrooms provided by the likes of Harvard,
Ohio University, the Australian Film TV and Radio School,
and New York University.

All sorts of companies have joined the crowd—for all sorts of reasons. Some are pitching or testing products. Starwood Hotels plans to open its new prototype, The Aloft, in 2008, and has built a virtual version in Second Life to get members' feedback on its design and features. It has sponsored concerts there to bring in visitors, most recently featuring Ben Folds, formerly the lead singer of the now-defunct Ben Folds Five.

Other companies are using Second Life as a meeting place where employees and managers from around the country or the world can gather away from the office while still sitting at their desks. At one virtual IBM session, avatars representing researchers in Australia, Florida, India, and Ireland hashed over supercomputing problems, instant messages bouncing back and forth. Thousands of IBM employees now have routine meetings on the site.

Advanced Micro Devices prides itself on being "a leading global provider of innovative processing solutions in the computing, graphics, and consumer electronics markets." In other words, it lives or dies by software developers. So it has created a pavilion in Second Life where developers, new and old, can network and attend lectures and training courses. It's located on the Second Life Developer Archipelago, and it includes an exhibition hall with interactive booths, scripted banners, and streaming videos.

Meanwhile, Linden Lab is not slowing down. In addition to instant messaging, the company now offers members the option of actually speaking to each other, using computer headsets. Not content with having established a virtual world built by the crowd, Linden has taken its crowdsourcing a step further.

WHAT YOU CAN DO

❖ **Get serious about the crowd.** When open sourcing first appeared, it was greeted mostly as a curiosity, certainly nothing that had a practical dollars-and-cents significance. When Second Life opened for business, hard-headed businesspeople  had pretty much the same reaction. No longer. The notion that the Internet crowds represent an important potential value beyond their role as customers has finally penetrated many corporate heads. How about yours?

❖ **Ask the right question.** If ever there was an example of the need to innovate these days, it has to be Second Life. The activities that some companies have undertaken are fascinating and make it clear that leaders have to find a way to expand their view of the possible. There are so many ways you haven't thought of to leverage your online community. One approach is to expand the universe of people you're depending upon for new ideas. Include everyone in the company, or all of your stakeholders (including investors), or all of your customers. One of your competitors might be taking those steps at this very moment. The question no longer is "What will they think of next?", but rather "How much time do we have before they think of it?"

It has released the code of its viewer application so that the online community of developers can improve it or add new features. No doubt, Second Life will be unrecognizable within another year or two.

A WORD FROM WE

"Feedback from stakeholders can create the innovation required to enter new markets or take over a larger market share."

—PETER TARHANIDIS

SugarCRM

This start-up in Cupertino, California, uses the power of community to create and continuously improve its open-source customer relationship management (CRM) software. Founder and CEO John Roberts describes it as "the collective work of bright CRM engineers around the world."

Before Roberts came along, open-source product development was limited to the infrastructure side of the IT market. Betting that a growing number of individual users and IT managers were fed up with having to pay big licensing fees for proprietary applications designed to help manage sales and keep tabs on customers, Roberts and his company offered customers free software, but with real people and their cache of knowledge standing by for support.

More than one million companies or individuals have
downloaded the software since the company released its
first version in April 2004, and any one of them can pitch in

to patch holes, fix errors,
provide more elegant
programming, or build
third-party extensions.
The open-source product
refinements and extensions
take place in what
the company calls the
SugarForge. Here interested
parties can see what kind
of functionality Sugar has
to offer at any given time. Sugar earns revenue by providing
technical support and customized versions of its software.

Some critics say Sugar's business model is confusing
and failure prone because it offers both an on-demand
subscription version of its software and the option of having
the program installed on in-house networks; either option
allows for customer modifications. Others scoff at the notion
that a significant number of corporate software buyers will
take a flyer on unknown open-source CRM applications.

But fans of Sugar counter that it is precisely the business
customers who are clamoring for less expensive choices that
can be customized to their particular needs
and wants. And even if the purchasing
executives themselves aren't savvy about
open sourcing, their IT departments
certainly are. Good reviews for Sugar will
filter up, they say.

Given that paying customers have migrated to Sugar over the past three years—all without any big and expensive corporate marketing campaigns—the proponents of the sweeter view seem to have the edge.

WHAT YOU CAN DO

❖ **Make sure everyone benefits.** It can be hard to get your business head around the idea that is so basic to crowdsourcing: Many members of the Internet community are happy to help you for free if you can create a situation that will satisfy  their needs or desires. SugarCRM has succeeded by doing just that, effectively turning over its software to the CRM community, urging its members to keep making the software better for their own sake, and then providing services built around the improved version. It's a righteous circle.

Virgin Mobile USA

The cell phone company uses 2,000 carefully selected online customers—"Insiders," as Virgin calls them—to keep it abreast of trends and promising opportunities. Virgin describes the group as "a team of elite,

Sir Richard Branson, founder and chairman of the Virgin Group, shows one of the first cell phones available from the leading U.S. wireless youth network Virgin Mobile USA.

young, and active customers," and it
rewards them with free calling minutes
and phone upgrades.

A joint venture of Richard Branson's
Virgin Group and Sprint Nextel, the
company goes to its Insider community—think: very hip
focus group—for help on everything from designing phones
to coming up with names for service plans. As one officer of
the company put it, "Ultimately, what we want to do is put
young consumers backstage."

But this is not high school, and being accepted as part of the
in-crowd is not the only way to be heard and earn rewards
at Virgin Mobile USA. The company, whose pay-as-you-go,
no-contract service has attracted 4.6 million phone users,
offers all of its mostly young Chatty Cathys and Texter
Thomases the chance to earn free phone minutes simply by
paying attention and giving feedback on a corporate sponsor's
advertisement. Any Virgin Mobile customer who watches
30-second commercials on his or her computer screen,
reads text messages on a cell phone, or fills out brand survey
questionnaires can earn up to 75 minutes a month of free
airtime. Called Sugar Mama, the program gives a notoriously
voluble group the chance to stay one step ahead of a dead cell
phone by voicing their opinions.

But more to the point, Sugar Mama enables sponsoring
partners to tap into the thoughts and opinions of a coveted
marketing segment, and they're happy to pay for the privilege.
As one corporate media director pointed out, knowing that
the kids don't get paid unless they watch an ad and answer
questions helps assure advertisers that they are getting
honest feedback.

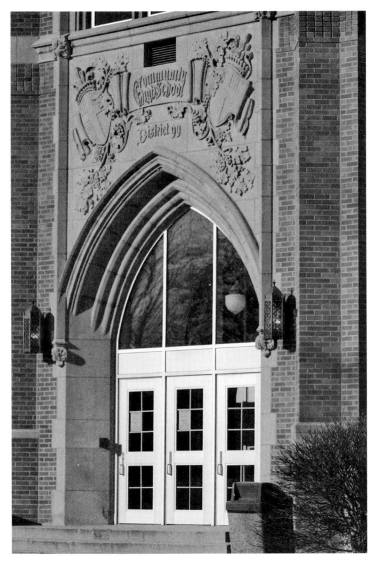

THIS IS NOT HIGH SCHOOL, AND BEING ACCEPTED AS PART OF THE IN-CROWD IS NOT THE ONLY WAY TO BE HEARD AND EARN REWARDS.

Catering to the crowd has also delivered an unexpected benefit to Virgin Mobile: buzz marketing. The kids are talking about the company, even those who use another network. When the company kicked off a clever text-messaging marketing program called Adopt-A-Mime that featured silent mimics in whiteface, the word spread fast, both in and out of the Virgin Mobile network. The buzz caused a notable number of non-Virgin customers to inquire about adopting a mime.

WHAT YOU CAN DO

❖ **Choose your partner.** In this chapter, we have been talking mostly about online communities numbering in the thousands or millions. But when you're looking for help in creating a new product or service, it could be more efficient and convenient to limit your reach to a portion of your potential community. That was the route Virgin Mobile took, narrowing its resource pool to just 2,000 of its best, brightest, and youngest.

WHAT YOU CAN DO

- ❖ **Spread the joy.** While concentrating on its Insider group, Virgin Mobile had the good sense not to deprive its other customers of a way to earn a reward. Had it not designed the Sugar Mama program for the masses, the bulk of its customers might have become resentful, thereby negating the Insider group's impact on product development. As it is, satisfaction surveys, such as those conducted by J. D. Power and Associates among wireless pre-paid customers and those conducted by Virgin Mobile USA among its own customers, put Virgin Mobile at the top of the heap.

- ❖ **Think almost free.** Sometimes you might actually want to pay the members of your community—not because they would otherwise refuse to help, but because it's a way to make them more committed to your cause. Free minutes and phone upgrades will not dent Virgin Mobile's bottom line, but they work wonders in convincing  the company's young customers to go "backstage." Of course, you need to be careful not to insult sophisticated volunteer members of your community with trinkets.

Idea Crossing

Fresh strategic ideas from fresh-faced MBA students—that's the product marketed by Idea Crossing, a Los Angeles start-up. Each year it runs the Innovation Challenge, a contest that tosses corporate problems into the laps of 3,000 of the brightest minds on college campuses around the world. Organizations ranging from the U.S. Postal Service to Hilton Hotels and Whirlpool pay $50,000 and up to sponsor the brain-bending competitions among school teams.

Founded in 2002 by Anil Rathi, then a gifted innovator himself at the Thunderbird School of Global Management, Idea Crossing initially hoped to link consumers who had come up with great product ideas to the companies that could bring the ideas to market. The competition started as something of an incidental experiment. But when the brainiacs leaped at the chance to tackle real-world problems and the companies swooned over the solutions these young outsiders came up with, the "experiment" graduated into the annual Innovation Challenge.

In the 2006 competition, a team from the Desautels Faculty of Management at McGill University in Montreal beat out 439 other teams of graduate students from 88 universities for top honors and a $20,000 prize. Its winning ideas centered on growth-enhancing partnerships for Hilton Hotels and ways to connect Chrysler with baby boomers. The strategic details are not for public consumption; they now become the intellectual property of the competition's sponsors.

The Bronfman Building, home of the
Desautels Faculty of Management.

WHAT YOU CAN DO

❖ **Decide who does what.** The scenario
is familiar. Your company recognizes a
promising new business idea, which you
adopt and develop.
Then along come the
entrepreneurs who have
sniffed out a new market.
They develop a different
spin on the idea, which
they offer to share with
you for a fee. Fair enough.
But the danger is that,
before you know it, you're relying entirely
on the entrepreneurs for new takes
on the idea—and you're starting to lose
your company's innovative chops for lack
of practice.

Business has only begun to tap
the infinite potential of online
communities as arbiters and creators
of new designs and products.
Variations on Second Life are popping
up all over, for example, offering
untold opportunities for companies
to interact with creative consumers in
new and different ways.

But the contributions of crowdsourcing to the bottom line
are by no means limited to product development. In the next
chapter, we describe how companies are using communities
to handle their customer service needs—and the risks and
rewards of that approach. We also explore the reasons so
many customers are so happy to help each other, for free.

03

How May We Help We?

Hokie 15 of Tigard, Oregon, had a question: "I just got my new Smokette. It seems a bit small. Has anyone sent theirs back to upgrade?"

So did Vizguy of Hunt$Vega$, otherwise known as Huntsville, Alabama: "Can I use the Cookshack smoker in my garage without posing a problem?"

JPSmokin of Boise, Idaho, meanwhile, was having a blast: "Thanks to everyone for all the advice, recommendations, and recipes," he wrote. "Picked up my new 008 smoker oven Saturday, and it hasn't been setting idle. Shoot, I haven't had this much fun since the boss's wife lost her swimsuit top at the company picnic."

"Clean up your own mess."
—ROBERT FULGHUM

Hour by hour, day by day, hundreds of online Cookshack customers sign onto its various forums to ask and answer questions about barbecue sauce (another product line), smoker and barbecue ovens, and cooking techniques. All this Internet jabber seems to work fine for all parties, but it does seem a tad incongruous, given the down-home subject and the fact that we're talking about an old-fashioned, low-tech kind of business.

For more than 40 years, Cookshack has been cranking out ovens for home and commercial use in a 21,000-square-foot factory in Ponca City, Oklahoma. It was founded by Gene Ellis, a businessman and inventor, and his wife, Judy. Gene got his inspiration watching neighbors try to turn old refrigerators into barbecue smokers. He built a cabinet and added a tray to hold smoldering wood chips, and Judy helped develop recipes for the company's sauces and meat rubs. After the Ellises' deaths in a 1985 boating accident, their son and daughter took over. The major claim they make for their company is that its machines make barbecue and smoked foods "without a lot of fuss." That's because the food is wood-cooked at a low temperature under static conditions with no through movement of air (which tends to dry meat) and no need for water pans (moisture stays in the oven).

Buyers of the ovens and smokers, which range from a model that holds 25 pounds of meat to one that can handle as much as 750 pounds, get a 30-day money-back guarantee and the promise of great after-  purchase support. (The Cookshack Web site proclaims that "the customer is [almost] always right.") Cookshack has 25 employees and actively encourages its customers to contact the company (its toll-free number appears prominently on every page of its Web site). The forums are an adjunct to its live customer service and are meant to provide a body of knowledge that couldn't be transmitted in a phone call and to provide assistance 24 hours a day, seven days a week. And they are clearly popular. A recent visit to the cooking-technique section revealed 1,196 topics and 10,126 posts. By creating a folksy, friendly site and designing forums and archives tailored to all tastes, the company has sold its customers on providing their own customer support.

All sorts of businesses are transferring much of the service function onto the shoulders of the customers themselves. Traditionally, of course, customers who had questions about a product—how to put it together, why it wasn't working properly, how to use it to the best advantage—would call the company's help line and talk with a customer service representative.

"All of our service representatives are helping other customers, but your call is very important to us. Please stay on the line. Your waiting time is approximately 32 minutes."

That's still possible, but it's not as easy as it used to be. Getting through to a service representative can take 30 minutes or more, and even then, customers are liable to get shifted from one level of expertise to another. Meanwhile, under pressure

to reduce costs, many businesses have begun charging substantial fees for telephone support. After the warranty on Dell computers expires, for instance, the company collects $39 for each tech support call unless the customer has paid $189 for a one-year service contract. Apple iMac customers get to purchase a three-year version for $169.

The alternative these companies offer is a visit to their online version of customer service. Typically, there is a FAQ page

and probably one or more forums where customers can pose a question and have it answered by others who volunteer their time and wisdom. Hokie 15, for example, was assured by Cookshack forum gurus that he could prepare all sorts of wonderful barbecue on his Smokette, and they even gave him some recipes to try. Vizguy was warned that he might be smoking himself along with his brisket if he cooked in the garage.

For companies that offer it, online support has been a double boon. They save money by freeing customer-service personnel for other work, while also building a cohesive, loyal community of repeat customers who can be tapped for other purposes—say, to test new products.

Why are advice-dispensing customers willing to devote their time, gratis, to improving Cookshack's bottom line—or that of any other business? One possible explanation is ego. As Bill Rose, founder and executive director of the Service and Support Professionals Association, noted not long ago,

"Most customers want to be seen as experts and recognized as gurus in their fields." We suspect that a number of people in customer-service communities simply enjoy interacting with other like-minded individuals and helping them solve their problems.

If you're a barbecue enthusiast, like the crowd that hangs out at the Cookshack site, what better way to pass the time than exchanging experiences and suggestions with fellow smokemeisters? (By the way, you don't need a cast of thousands to advise customers online. Just 1 or 2 percent of the customer base can handle the job, according to Ron Munz, chief executive officer of the Help Desk Institute, an information technology trade association.)

Shifting service to a customer community raises some interesting questions, though. For one—and this is a biggie—how can you be sure that customers will provide the right answers? Suppose that, instead of elaborating on the Smokette's virtues, someone tells Hokie 15 that his oven is too small and then recommends a competitor's product? Can you trust your community to send defective product cases or billing problems directly to your service representatives rather than trying to deal with the customers online? In fact, where should the line be drawn between the two kinds of customer service?

Those are among the questions addressed by the following examples.

Netflix

Along with its inviting online presentation and oh-so-efficient distribution system, this booming movie-rental company prides itself on its capability to offer subscribers a compact list of films they are likely to enjoy watching.

"Imagine that our Web site was a brick-and-mortar store," Netflix vice president James Bennett told the *Los Angeles Times*. "When people walk through the door, they see the DVDs rearrange themselves. The movies that might interest them fly onto the shelves, and all the rest go to the back room."

In the real world, the movies don't do the rearranging; that's handled by the customers themselves, with an assist from a computer program called Cinematch. Customers are invited to rate each Netflix film they watch on a scale from 1 to 5. Cinematch digests these ratings, searches through the 80,000 titles in inventory, and comes up with a list of films tailored to the taste of each of the company's six million subscribers. By enticing them to rate films, Netflix achieves the latest in business magic tricks, getting customers to serve themselves.

The use of so-called recommenders is hardly unique to Netflix. Other online retailers, such as Amazon, Apple, eBay, and Overstock, rely on their customers for a helping hand in predicting what products the customers will prefer, whether bedding, books, CDs, or DVDs.

Customer ratings are used to rank corporate service providers as well.

For all these companies, the recommender system offers more than the chance to provide an extra service. It helps them establish a stronger connection with customers. Studies have shown that it can substantially increase online sales.

The extent of Netflix's commitment to personalized movie recommendations was made clear in November 2006 when the company offered a $1 million prize—in true wikinomics spirit—to anyone who can build a system that is at least 10 percent better at the job than Cinematch. The competition is to end in

2011. Meanwhile, Netflix has enticed many of the leading lights in the field of artificial intelligence to join in. Among the contestants' discoveries to date: For reasons unknown, most Netflix subscribers share the same attitude toward *The Wizard of Oz* and *Silence of the Lambs*.

The company has made yet another bow to crowdsourcing with a feature called Friends. It enables subscribers to see each other's list of films watched, to compare the ratings they have awarded the films, and to exchange suggestions for other films to watch. Once again, the crowd is invited to play a role in customer service.

Bradbury Software

In his office in Nashville, Tennessee, home of the Grand Ole Opry, Nick Bradbury was a one-man band. The company's only employee, he sort of liked the solitary life.

WHAT YOU CAN DO

❖ **Save!** On average, telephone customer support costs a company $25 to $50 a call; even e-mails run $4 to $15 per contact. That should be enough to inspire you to consider getting your company's community to take on part of the support job. As Netflix discovered with its recommender program, a community's services are often virtually free.

❖ **Promote!** Even though its personalized recommendations are so important in the Netflix scheme of things, they are not promoted on the company's "Welcome" and "How It Works" pages. So unless you go deeper into the site and become a member, you never learn about the rating system and the part it plays in nominating films you'll really like. That goes for the Friends feature as well. If you want your customers to serve themselves and you want potential customers to know about the value that creates, make sure you let them know up front and personal.

WHAT YOU CAN DO

❖ **Reward!** Netflix's decision to offer a prize for a system that outmatches Cinematch is a reminder that rewards are potent energizers for customers engaged in service and support functions. One effective approach is to have customers rank those customers who help them, and then award them special status of some kind—a symbol next to their icon, for example—and/or small items bearing the company logo.

After graduating from the University of Tennessee, he tried to make a living as a cartoonist. His comic strip, about a koala bear named Basil, poked fun at everything from politicians to television commercials. Then Bradbury took up computer programming, another solitary occupation, eventually creating the HTML editor, Homesite, which he sold in 1996. Two years later, he founded Bradbury Software and all by himself developed FeedDemon, a news aggregator, and TopStyle, a Web design program.

Bradbury's products were selling well, but he had a problem. When it came to customer support, his company was off-

key. There was no way he could keep up with customers' questions and occasional complaints, so

he handed over the job to the customers themselves. On
the Bradbury Web site, he set up a customer-to-customer
forum, a so-called peer support group where more than 2,000
people provided the after-purchase service he couldn't handle
himself.

In May 2005, Bradbury Software was acquired by NewsGator
Technologies, based in Denver, and Nick Bradbury was
hired and given the title "Architect,
Client Products." In other words,
he continues to spend hours alone,
thinking about new ways to improve
his two products. He also regularly
visits the forums on the NewsGator
Web site to check out product
suggestions his customers offer.

Like many other technical sites,
NewsGator offers three levels of
service and support. It asks customers
to start by searching its extensive knowledge base because
that's where answers to most questions can be found. If
that doesn't work, the customer is urged to move on to
the NewsGator forums, where veteran customers provide
answers. The third option is traditional: Customers can e-mail
the company's support staff.

To make sure the Bradbury products' customer service is
properly maintained, NewsGator decided to hire a new
customer service manager. It started by looking close to home
and found just the right person: Jack Brewster, a customer
who had been a major contributor on the original Bradbury
forums. You can take the boy out of the Bradbury, but you
can't take the Bradbury out of the boy.

WHAT YOU CAN DO

- **Ride herd.** The benefits of turning over a portion of the service function to customers are substantial, but so are the dangers. Those expert customers could be handing out inexpert answers. Follow Nick Bradbury's example and make sure you "check out" your customer forums on a regular basis.

- **Get organized.** As the NewsGator approach suggests, a high-traffic support Web site should give the customer-in-need more than a single option. Questions and answers should be analyzed and organized in an archive or knowledge base. Many customers prefer using such a system—the same folks who would rather use an ATM than deal with a bank teller. That's good news because it means that your customers who man the forums have more time to deal with problems. By the way, those volunteers should be encouraged to become experts in navigating the archive so they can use it to make sure they're handing out the right skinny.

PMI Audio Group

Around the same time Nick Bradbury began his solitary life as a computer programmer in Tennessee, Alan Hyatt, one-time professional guitarist, was setting up PMI Audio Group, a California-based distributor of professional audio equipment. He called his company a group, but, like Bradbury, he was the only employee. Today PMI is still a distributor, handling recording, video, film, broadcast, and other products. But now it owns most of the businesses whose products it sells. That means PMI must concern itself with matters most distributors don't have to worry about: product design, manufacturing, marketing, and customer service.

To cope with customer service, the company relies, in part, on its online forums where old hands instruct newbies on the intricacies of such complex topics as multipattern diaphragm condensers, dual-channel mic, precompressor EQ, and ATB mixers. The discussions of technical issues turned out to be so detailed and to the point that the company archived them on its Web site, organized according to product, and directed customers with questions to check them out as a first step toward finding answers.

PMI reaps rewards beyond the customer service function. When numbers of people began talking about a product on the Web site, they became a cohesive and loyal community. When the company has a problem with, say, quality control, these folks are the first to be supportive. They also share their ideas for new or improved product lines—and alert the company when a new product fails to measure up. That

 happened with PMI's ATB mixer, which started out with four auxiliary send channels. The forum members protested that more were needed, and the company responded by redesigning the product to include six channels instead of four.

In 2006, a hacker wreaked havoc with PMI'S forums, and Alan Hyatt had to shut them down and start all over again, rebuilding from scratch. No fun. The strength of the Internet is its openness and lack of restraints, but those very strengths leave online communities prey to Internet predators. They are an infinitesimal minority of the online crowd, but as in so many areas of life, one rotten apple can do a lot of damage.

Intuit

When this financial software powerhouse set up shop in 1984, its first product was Quicken, which has now been purchased by more people than all other personal finance software items combined. Two decades later, Quicken's parent company, Intuit, decided to test the idea of customer-support forums, but it wanted to avoid the hassles of building and managing them. So it turned to LiveWorld, a specialist in creating, operating, and moderating social networks and online communities.

The Quicken forums are organized according to products and computer type, PC or Mac. Other customers quickly answer Quicken queries, usually in helpful detail. In fact, the company says that volunteers answer 70 percent of all support questions, taking an enormous load off customer

WHAT YOU CAN DO

❖ **Rate the experts.** When the product is complex, as is the case with PMI, the demands on customer forum personnel are greater—and so is the need to maintain constant surveillance. The  surest way is to ask visitors to the site to rate the solutions they receive. Forum volunteers who consistently earn low scores should be replaced; as mentioned earlier, those who receive consistently high scores should be in line for rewards.

❖ **Bring in the pros.** By surveying questions and answers in the customer forums and in e-mails and calls to office staff, you should be able to spot problems that are causing customer experts the most difficulty. Organize occasional tutorials whereby the staff can provide the right answers to these and any other problems the volunteers are experiencing.

service employees. For example, when ten-year customer "Allan" complained that some of his mutual fund data wasn't showing in a Quicken capital gains report, several other customers began a dialogue. Some wrote lengthy explanations of the entire capital-gains process, and all offered the kind of caveats most employees would shun.

Of course, LiveWorld and its competitors charge for their services. Whether a company wants to take that route to get customers to serve themselves depends on its culture, finances, and technical savvy. But it's an option that a number of major companies, including America Online, Campbell Soup, Dove, and MINI Cooper, have embraced.

In the chapter just ahead, we examine what might seem to be the most unlikely of all crowdsourcing applications: the use of a customer community to sell products and services to its members and to consumers. Yet, as you will see, the logic behind the approach is unassailable. In fact, major corporations have begun to follow that route and are achieving major breakthroughs in sales and profits.

WHAT YOU CAN DO

* **Check your ego at the (virtual) door.** Inevitably, forum volunteers will come up against questions they can't answer. Your job is to make sure they quickly move the question to higher authority, whether by e-mail or by phone. Volunteers need to be drilled in the philosophy that the ultimate goal is to solve customer problems, and individual egos should never get in the way.

* **Talk straight.** "Allan," the Quicken customer mentioned earlier, reaped one of the major benefits of the online service forums: the willingness of the customer experts to mention product weaknesses. Of course, none of your employee experts is going to go on record criticizing your company's products. But as you know, what counts above all if you want to keep his or her business is that the customer be treated well and fairly.

04

Customer, Sell Thyself

Yes, Procter & Gamble is in the business of turning out consumer products by the barrelful. As its Web site boasts, "Three billion times a day P&G brands touch the lives of people around the world." But the company has another, very different line of business as well. It offers up the services of hundreds of thousands of moms and teenagers as word-of-mouth marketers—for its own product divisions and those of other organizations as well.

Donna Wetherell, of Columbus, Ohio, is one of those "mom connectors," as they're called. She's employed at a customer service call center, where she's known as "the coupon lady." That's because she's always passing out P&G coupons and sharing news of new products with her 300 coworkers. They enjoy her visits, too.

"Dollars alone don't build a brand."

—ROBERT J. DAVIS

All of us like to chat about the goods we buy and use. Each week, the average person mentions specific brands 56 times in the course of 100 conversations. And studies have shown that today's consumers rely far more on what their friends and colleagues have to say about a product than on the ads they see on television. That's why, whether in person, on the phone, or online, the messages carried by Donna Wetherell and her connector colleagues are so often welcome. "We know," says Steve Knox, chief executive officer of Vocalpoint, "that the most powerful form of marketing is an advocacy message from a trusted friend."

P&G's word-of-mouth operation has two distinct pieces: Vocalpoint and Tremor. The Vocalpoint unit focuses primarily on P&G products and boasts 500,000 mothers who have children under 19. The Tremor unit focuses mainly on products from clients other than P&G and includes 250,000 teenagers. Proprietary research techniques enabled the company to find teens and moms who are gregarious and rich in friends. The average teenager has 25 friends on her instant message buddy list, while teen connectors have 150 or so. Mom connectors talk to 25 or so people a day, versus 5 for the average mother.

When P&G set about introducing its new dishwashing detergent, Dawn Direct Foam, it hired Vocalpoint to organize a crowdsourcing campaign. This is how Steve Knox describes what happened next: "Our connector moms looked at this product and went, 'Wow! That's so cool. My kids would want to help.'" That reaction led Knox to establish the talking points for his word-of-mouth army. In discussions with friends and colleagues, they would offer some "helpful hints" on how to get kids to do more chores around the house.

After that, Knox explains, "Dawn became a natural part of the conversation." The results: "We nearly doubled Dawn's business in the test market."

In 2005 the milk industry was preparing a national campaign to convince teenagers to forego sodas and drink milk as a way to reduce weight and body fat. Tremor's piece of it was to use word-of-mouth marketing to get teens who were drinking one glass of milk a day to drink more.

Teen connectors were sent a mailer that listed the benefits of drinking three glasses of milk a day ("achieve the look you want") and white "3X/day" bracelets to share with friends. In phone and e-mail messages, the connectors urged people to sign up for the 3X Challenge, offering them a chance to download a diary to keep track of their progress. Those who did received a cup and a bracelet by mail. The results: In no time, the effort had 1.5 million teenagers talking about milk. And according to

Tom Nagle, senior vice president of the International Dairy Food Association, "We were able to measure big increases in consumption in test versus control markets."

What started at P&G as a means to better peddle its own products has now become a profit center with clients ranging from cereal maker Kashi to cable channel Animal Planet to lubricant manufacturer WD-40. "We know," says Knox, "that the most powerful form of marketing is an  advocacy message from a trusted friend." Or as P&G's CEO A. G. Lafley likes to say, "The consumer has become the marketer."

"Next to doing the right thing, the most important thing is to let people know you are doing the right thing."

—JOHN D. ROCKEFELLER

Procter & Gamble's success with word-of-mouth sales is just one example—although an impressive one—of the role this revolutionary breed of crowdsourcing can play in a marketing program. We use *revolutionary* advisedly. After all,  merchants have relied on their customers to "spread the word" about their goods at least since the earliest Egyptians bartered their grain for olive oil or honey in the markets of Memphis. It's just that mobilizing huge numbers of people to take on that task, and paying them nothing or next to nothing to do so, puts a whole new, directed spin on an old, spontaneous practice.

By far the majority of P&G's connectors are upbeat about its products, but, of course, there are no controls on what they actually say. Some comfort can be found in studies that show that when Americans talk about brands, positive mentions outnumber negative by 6 to 1.

In the balance of this chapter, we offer more examples of the community as salesperson, along with some suggestions for how you can put all those people to work in your behalf.

M80

Back in 1998, Dave Neupert had an idea he thought would eventually be heard loud and clear in the marketing world. That's why he called his new company M80 Interactive Marketing, after the big-bang daddy of all firecrackers.

The story opens two years earlier, when Neupert was working at a record company in Los Angeles and eager to promote his clients through the Internet. He began setting up Web sites for bands, including one for the Deftones. It was the company's first with a chat room, and Neupert soon realized that a community of enthusiastic fans was forming around the site. Many of them complained that the band's music wasn't being played much on the radio. Neupert suggested they mobilize, using the Internet to spread the word. They did, and in short order, Deftones record sales started to rise.

Neupert got the message—and founded M80. Then, as now, the company followed a basic three-step formula:

1. Find rabid fans of the band, TV show, or whatever product he was promoting.

2. Convince them to push the product online, pretty much gratis.

3. Teach them how to go about it.

The fans he pursued were primarily young, and the products he asked them to push were those that had some cult popularity among the young. In an early interview, he described the crowdsourcing campaign he ran in 1999 to promote a new album for the band *NSYNC. The volunteer online crew consisted of 4,000 people, mainly teenage girls. "We build huge blitz teams, as we like to call them," he says. They were urged to go onto  Web sites where music fans congregated, including those of radio stations, to spread the word that a new *NSYNC album was due to hit the street shortly. "These fans are competitive in the boy-band community," according to Neupert. "They wanted to beat the Backstreet Boys' first-week sales record. We spread that word to fans that we had to beat that record."

A WORD FROM WE

"With communication costs decreasing, feedback has become significantly more cost effective. Hundreds of thousands of discussion groups, rating systems, e-mail threads, and blogs offer completely unsolicited complaints, comments, and advice for every product known to man."

—DONNA PITTERI, MEMBER OF THE WE ARE SMARTER COMMUNITY

Then and now, M80 feeds its teams "inside" information about client tours or videos and the date an ad campaign is due to kick off. Knowing when radio stations are going to carry promotions for a band, for example, can spur a team to greater efforts. "We tell them, 'Let's drive the spins up,'" he says. Core team members are rewarded with T-shirts, tickets, and other items.

Since the early days, the company has spread its wings. It has helped some 150 clients including many outside the music industry, such as Comedy Central, The Gap, Tommy Hilfiger, Honda, Napa Auto Parts, Cingular Wireless, and Fox Broadcasting. Revenues rose to $2 million a year.

Whether Neupert will be able to take his technique into the realms of less exotic products—toilet paper leaps to mind—remains to be seen. He's optimistic. "Everyone is passionate about something," he told the *Los Angeles Times*. "But we need to harness that enthusiasm."

Meanwhile, he's not lacking for admirers in the marketing world. In 2006, WPP Group, the giant marketing and communications firm, acquired 51 percent of M80's stock. No price was announced, but the sale demonstrated conclusively that the leveraging of the online community for product sales had come of age.

WHAT YOU CAN DO

❖ **Know your fans.** Chances are, you're not in the music business—or sports or film, for that matter—so your customers are unlikely to be so fanatic about your product. That means you will need to do

some extra research to spot those you can inspire to become your new, auxiliary sales staff. Tap your marketing people to find customers who have called or written praising the product and those who have a long track record of purchasing it. Contact these customers directly with an invitation to join an elite club of advisor-connectors. You can also issue a general invitation via your Web site.

WHAT YOU CAN DO

❖ **Make them happy.** The trinkets and other freebies that P&G and M80 hand out are not the major attraction for word-of-mouth volunteers. They like being able to get across their point of view to other customers and to the companies' management as well. They enjoy being on the inside. When M80 was hired to promote a new DVD of the TV cartoon "The Family Guy," which had recently been taken off the air, Dave Neupert learned that fans of the show objected strongly to its cancellation. "We're trying to persuade fans to help us promote, and they're trying to use us to talk to the show's producers," he says. Inspired in part by M80's findings, the network brought the show back to life.

MasterCard

The advertising side of marketing has also tapped the online community for help in selling services and products. A pioneer in that regard was MasterCard, which invited visitors to its Web site to create their own versions of the highly successful "priceless" ads. Winners have been aired on television and posted on the www.priceless.com site, where visitors

are urged to vote for their favorites. Although no cash prizes were offered, the contest drew more than 100,000 entries.

A recent incarnation of the priceless promotion was a contest for college students, inviting them to write an essay and create a video about some aspect of their hometown that would make people want to visit. The winner was to spend the summer traveling around the world visiting some of these "priceless" places.

According to Joyce King Thomas, chief creative officer of MasterCard's advertising agency, McCann Erickson, "The campaign was interactive from the beginning. People wrote their own posters, made their own films, and did parodies."

Thomas and MasterCard could not have been thrilled by the parodies, thousands of which flooded Web sites; many of them were profane or obscene. "You're tapping into that consumer desire to have a piece of it," says Lawrence Flanagan, executive vice president and chief marketing officer at MasterCard worldwide. "You have to take the good with the bad."

In another contest tapping the online community, this time sponsored by USA Network, visitors to the company Web site were urged to upload videos of themselves as potential characters on USA Network shows; the winner appeared in a commercial and in an online series. The goal, according to Chris McCumber, a marketing vice president, was to allow members of the network's community to be "a part of the brand."

WHAT YOU CAN DO

❖ **Tap the talent.** Any sizeable community has large numbers of talented people—writers, artists, photographers—who are eager to see their work on display. When they invited their communities to create and upload videos, MasterCard and USA Network were well aware that a substantial number of the entries would be of little quality and less value. But they wanted to get these contestants to help in the process of binding customers and potential customers to their products and organizations. And they succeeded.

❖ **Narrow the target.** To reduce the number of off-subject and off-color videos uploaded, Yahoo! reached out to customers of a particular brand rather than the whole world of its Web site. Yahoo! Music urged fans of Shakira to turn out their own version of her video "Hips Don't Lie" and avoided the "priceless" problem. "I call it participation marketing," says Cammie Dunaway, chief marketing officer for Yahoo!. "Allow them to help you shape the brand experience."

> "Never write an advertisement which
> you wouldn't want your family to read.
> You wouldn't tell lies to your own wife.
> Don't tell them to mine."
>
> —DAVID OGILVY, LEGENDARY ADMAN

Circuit City, Overstock.com, Macy's, Sears, and More

The list of companies that have opened their Web pages to customer product reviews grows daily—and, on the face of it, that's pretty strange. Question: Since when have business leaders been willing to countenance, much less sponsor, the appearance of negative as well as positive comments about their products in public? Answer: Since they began to recognize that their customers wanted to speak their minds about products they care about. And since they learned that authentic customer reviews lure serious spenders to their sites and increase sales.

One 2006 study found that 77 percent of Internet shoppers depended upon customer reviews, and half described the reviews as "critical" to their purchases. In other words, members of the communities of customers at these stores are telling other customers which products to buy, and the other customers are buying them—a prime instance of crowdsourcing as marketing tool.

Along with the proliferation of customer product reviews on merchant Web sites has come a variety of independent third-party sites that offer the same service. Each provides a somewhat different spin.

Reevoo.com, for example, works directly with some of Great Britain's largest online retailers, such as Dixons and Jessops. It contacts people who have made a purchase at one of those sites and asks them to give the item a mark from 1 to 10 in assorted categories of interest.

One of the charms of the Reevoo site is that reviews on quality, ease of use, and the like are shown as they are written by the customer so the visitor gets all sorts of down-to-earth, practical comments—"The screen  scratches very easily," for example, or "The camera is a silly shape to have swinging round your neck."

When we visited the site, we found that Colin of Newcastle Upon Tyne had given his new Samsung HDTV-ready, LCD model a 9 (as did seven out of eight others surveyed, by the way), saying the picture and sound quality were "excellent." However, "by the time the TV [was] fully set up," Colin warned, the "stand had become rocky even when [the] fittings [were] re-tightened." Besides Colin's Samsung report, more than 300 other television reviews were listed, covering 38 brands.

Clicking on "Vacuum Cleaners" brought up 116 reviews of 20 brands, including one by David from Glasgow, who wasn't all that thrilled with the Bosch model he had chosen. David gave it a 3, citing a "poorly designed bagless dust box" that "clogs up very quickly (a sweet wrapper can foul it 100 percent)." He went on to say that the thing was "difficult to empty, and the plastic tags have broken already."

Other Bosch models ranked much higher with those who volunteered their opinions.

Reevoo emphasizes that, unlike product reviews on other sites, such as Amazon, its system virtually weeds out spam and overly flattering comments from the manufacturer disguised as unbiased customer comments. The company never pays its reviewers, on the theory that when money changes hands, bias can sneak in and compromise the quality of the appraisal.

Reevoo, which was founded in 2004, collects a fee from its partner retailers for being able to display the ReevooMark on their Web sites. As of spring 2007, the company had carried 60 million reviews and ratings.

! A WORD FROM WE

"Historically, people have gathered in marketplaces to swap stories and goods. This perspective got lost during the rise of mass production and mass communication. The Web brings it back. Today successful marketing depends not only on broadcast and reach, but also on word-of-mouth—the high-tech equivalent of the human conversations in a souk, bazaar, or general store porch."

—GROUP CONTRIBUTION

Angieslist.com, based in Indianapolis, charges its 500,000 members $10 to join and $6 a month for the privilege of

reading other members' reviews of local service businesses, from plumbers and electricians to nail parlors and dogwalkers. It has chapters in more than 100 cities.

Other privileges of Angie's List membership include a local monthly magazine (which evolved from a newsletter), discounts at some companies, and a call-in service to help find the right provider in an emergency, such as with a broken water pipe. On the basis of their individual experience, members rate a service provider from A to F on such factors as price, quality, punctuality, and responsiveness. They also fill out reports describing the particular job, which can be most revealing. One comment by a member who hired someone to prepare a home for sale, including painting, plaster work, and new flooring: "What was to be a 3- to 5-day job turned into a 37-day nightmare."

The founder of the site, Angie Hicks, has spent more than a decade organizing what she calls a homeowners' grapevine online. When members are looking for, say, a roofer, they can click on that category for a list of local roofers that have been rated, along with such data as their current grade and whether they offer any Angie's List discounts. Clicking on the individual company name opens a full profile.

WHAT YOU CAN DO

❖ **Honesty pays.** Enticing your online community to write customer reviews of your products can deliver a powerful marketing tool, but it can quickly turn sour if customers suspect you've planted all those positive reviews. Overstock.com had that sort of problem: Customer reviewers wanted to know why their upbeat comments were showing up on the site, but not their negative ones. It turned out that the critical comments were being deep-sixed by managers in charge of the under-the-gun product lines. (Incidentally, Overstock leveraged its review system by stocking up on and promoting items that got very high ratings.) If you open your site to customer reviewers, you have to be willing to take the negative with the positive—that's the trade-off for gaining the trust and loyalty of your customers.

WHAT YOU CAN DO

❖ **Make your (multiple) choice.** If you
   want to include customer reviews in your
   company's operations,
   you can go in two basic
   directions: Hire an outsider
   or go it alone. Using an
   outsider risks losing
   control of the process,
   so you would have to set
   up mechanisms within
   your company to closely
   supervise your supplier.
   Going it alone requires that you have
   employees assigned to your Web site who
   can be counted on to monitor comments
   for irrelevant or objectionable content
   while making sure not to lose negative
   reviews. The success of a review page rests
   in part on the clarity and completeness of
   the introduction and explanations. In that
   regard, we tilt toward getting best-practice
   advice from outside experts.

The growth and public popularity of customer reviews and
the other examples of crowdsource marketing speak directly
to a basic change in the nature of the relationship between
you and your customer. The old commercial model in which
you presented the products for sale and the customer simply
chose among them is fast eroding. Today the customer is

increasingly calling the shots. She's telling the world whether
she likes or hates particular products she's tried. If you invite
her, she's also up for making
a few suggestions on how you
might improve a product.
Tomorrow she will insist on
your coming up with new
products that precisely meet
her taste, telling you how
they should be marketed and
distributed, and proclaiming
how well you've handled those tasks.

You can try to hold back the tide, maintaining your old way
of doing business. You can find out what the customer wants
and provide it. Or, best of all, you can determine where she's
headed and get there ahead of her.

In the next chapter, we explore another area in which
the community is altering traditional business patterns:
manufacturing. In company after company, the crowd is
actually producing the organization's product—and doing a
great job of it.

If We Build It, We Will Come

There was a time—just a few years ago, really—when thousands of highly skilled, professional photographers counted on the licensing of their work by stock photo houses to pay a big chunk of their rent. Not anymore. A lethal combination of new technology and crowdsourcing is doing them in.

This is the way it used to work: To illustrate their wares, magazines, ad agencies, corporate publications, and film companies routinely turned to photo agencies that stored collections of shots by professionals. Customers might have to pay fees of $100 or more for the one-time use of a photo, but that was still a lot cheaper than assigning a photographer to do the job. As magazine circulations declined and ad budgets were cut, the fees fell, too, but they still provided a safety net for the pros in an increasingly unstable business.

Enter the digital camera. Suddenly, anyone with a semblance of skill was able to produce accurate, attractive images. If the first shot didn't work, you could always keep trying until it did. And when you learned how to use

"Snowflakes are a fragile thing, but look at what they can do when they stick together."

—FERNANDO BONAVENTURA

Photoshop, you could make your image even better. If you had enough friends with digital cameras, you didn't need to hire a professional photographer to record your wedding, birthday, or family reunion.

Enter crowdsourcing. With all those millions of people clicking away on their digital cameras, millions of images were sitting around on computers. Most of the photos weren't professional quality, but there were an awful lot of good shots just taking up space. So it wasn't long before microstock houses, as they're known, began to appear on the Internet to tap that huge  supply of digital images. The newcomers charged customers as little as $1 for a royalty-free license.

The pioneer was Calgary-based iStockphoto, which giant Getty Images bought in 2006 for $50 million. The iStock library holds more than 1.7 million images from 36,000  members, and it has been blessed with Getty's advanced search and index technology, which makes it much easier for customers around the world to find just what they're looking for. The photos might not be up to the quality you'll find at Getty Images itself, but they have been selected by the company's editors, so they're apt to be just fine if you're putting together an office newsletter or even a magazine spread. And the price will be right.

iStock introduced a payment system that has become the industry standard. The minimum purchase is $12, which gives you 10 credits; images cost between 1 and 15 credits per download. The prices rise with the image size and resolution. iStock photos are downloaded at the rate of one every 2.5 seconds.

One reason for the site's success has been its welcoming content from contributors. The images are accompanied by symbols indicating how many of their photos have been sold through iStock and whether the work has been chosen for special attention on the site. Articles on the site offer photographic and design advice, and forums enable contributors to exchange news and speak their minds. The royalties many receive are impressive— exclusive contributors earn, on average, $1,000 a month. Also, they're happy about having other people see their work.

In this chapter, our focus is on the role of communities in manufacturing companies' products or, as in the case of iStock, content. The advantages over traditional business models are huge. At iStock, for instance, contributors not only create the product being sold, but they also deliver it

in a market-ready format and list it in the appropriate keyword category. With little or no product inventory expense or traditional overhead, the company can price the product far below that of old-model competitors.

Here are some more examples of crowdsourcing at work providing companies with their content. We hope the variety will suggest how close to infinite are its potential applications—within your company or any company you might choose to create. And take note: We haven't even included Wikipedia.

Zebo.com

Joanna Z's fondest hopes and dreams, she tells her friends on Zebo.com, include owning a pair of thousand-dollar Lanvin pumps. When she sees something else she covets, she drools—and types, "Look at that conical black heel. Sigh."

Zebo, one of a growing number of so-called social shopping sites, is home to more than five million young and some not-so-young materialists. They travel from one member's page to another, taking in each other's photographs, profiles, blogs, and lists of products desired and products possessed. By and large, they are not searching out people for their character traits or even their looks; it's their belongings that count. And

if by chance all that window-shopping brings on a buying urge, it can be satisfied at ZeboShops, an e-commerce page just a click away.

Launched in 2006 by Roy de Souza, a veteran marketing strategist, Zebo bills itself as "the world's largest repository of what people own." It reflects de Souza's conviction that young people today are what they own. "They list things because it defines them," he says.

Most members range between the ages of 16 and 25, although there are kids as young as 13 and some five times

that age. Take "Sircharlie M, 63, divorced," who says he owns a house, a 2004 Chevy truck, and eight remote-controlled aircraft that he built himself. Now Sircharlie is hoping to find "a nice lady to date."

There are all sorts of other things to find. Under "Celebrity Profiles," you can see "what the stars own and want, as reported by them!"

Mike James, for one, a point guard who in 2007 signed a four-year, $23-million contract with the NBA's Minnesota Timberwolves, listed a plasma television, a Playstation, soul food, Mexican food, chicken noodle soup, two pit bulls, tattoos, a Lincoln Navigator, and a Maserati among his possessions. His wish list includes "lots of video games," a Nissan Quest, and a Ford F-250 truck.

At the ZEBuzz forum, you can have real-time conversations "with other people who are bored, too!" You can start a group of your own about anything you want.

Product information of sorts can be found on ZE'Answers, where members pose and respond to shopping- and product-related questions. One day, Taylor asked about the most popular cell phone color. Eighty-six people replied to Taylor, including one who didn't actually own a cell phone but offered this comment: "Who cares what color it is, as long as it works good? A nonworking phone isn't worth having."

Zebo.com does not enable e-mail blocking, a red flag for some parent groups worried about cyberstalkers or cyberbullies

pursuing young members. Other critics say that boasting online about owning expensive cars, audio and visual equipment, jewelry, and the like is like giving a burglar your house keys and leaving the light on for him.

But it seems more likely that Zebo members will become the targets of marketers rather than burglars. Regular visitors to the site willingly provide reams of information about their product preferences and buying habits, marketable data that is easily accessible to everyone. That has not escaped the notice of de Souza, who is also the CEO and cofounder of Zedo Inc., a Silicon Valley Internet ad serving business.

Under the heading "See New Stuff," which
pitches "cool new products from many stores,"
members and visitors are linked to thousands
of items that they are encouraged to rate, blog
about, add to their wish lists, or buy outright. A
foray into this section turned up everything from a $3 "Scotty
Greeting Card from Coi" to a $425 ruby. Clicking on a picture
of a product brings up a rating bar and the question "Is this
[item] in or out?" The viewer then has the option of ranking
the item on a scale of 1 to 10.

There are unofficial merchants as well. Brenda, a self-
identified 52-year-old divorcee, lists 19 items she owns and
lusts for more, particularly from French fashion designer
Louis Vuitton. But if you scroll down to "Brenda's Zebo blog,"
you discover that she is, in fact, a reseller of trendy designer
merchandise, "straight from the factory floor," which she's
selling for "even less than wholesale!!!!!" Her business Web
sites and a phone number are provided.

Whatever you may think of connecting people via their
materialistic yearnings, you have to admit that de Souza has
found an ingenious means of getting a huge community of
mainly young people to supply him with content that draws
ever more of them to his site. That's what crowdsourcing is all
about.

ThisNext.com

As with Zebo, ThisNext relies on members
to create its content—namely, lists of their
favorite products. Also, like Zebo, ThisNext
provides links to stores.

WHAT YOU CAN DO

- **Get emotional.** What makes Zebo.com and so many other community-driven sites successful is its basic premise: Young people are passionate about possessions, those they own and those they want. That's an important message for anyone thinking about using crowdsourcing as a manufacturing process. The crowd will not come to you unless you touch them where they live. No one wants to devote time and dollars to a site about your new brand of aspirin; a site dedicated to exchanging news and views about pain control is more likely to succeed.

- **Get the crowd involved.** As the Zebo site suggests, the more ways you can provide visitors with a chance to express themselves, the more likely they will hang around and identify with your operation. Forums, targeted question-and-answer pages, ratings systems—they're all calculated to keep members busy and involved and eager to keep delivering up more content. It's a virtuous circle.

When you enter the name of an item in the search bar, you
end up on pages with a variety of nominations and links
to the nominators. We typed in
"surfboard," for example, and
discovered 22 options, from
miniature surfboard towel
hooks ("They brighten up a kid's
bathroom," wrote Jody) to a Rusty
shortboard ("Thin as a chip, turny
but definitely not a flip flopper,"
according to Allyson). In each case, we were informed how
many members recommended an item and what tags were
applicable to the choice ("waves," "Venice"). We were also told
where the item could be purchased.

ThisNext, once again like Zebo, is known as a social shopping
site. It enables its members to create their own pages with
a photo, a profile, and answers to a long series of questions,
such as "What is the next big step you'd like to
make?" It also allows them to go to other
members' blogs to find more examples of
their product tastes or simply to establish
contact. And although the member lists
on ThisNext are weighted toward products, they can range far
and wide, from activities (cooking and climbing, for example)
to entertainment (movie reviews), to lifestyles (living green).

In theory, everyone posting products is a private citizen, but
it's easy for a company's employees to sign up as individuals
and promote the company's product. Some consultants
actually advise clients to do so as a means of "building buzz"
around a product. Still, such recommendations are in the
minority. As a member told the *New York Times,* "I like the
concept of peers, people like me, referring each other to
interesting things. It's more trustworthy."

WHAT YOU CAN DO

❖ **Shrug.** When you open yourself to the crowd, you will inevitably find some people eager to exploit your site for their own ends. In the case of ThisNext, for example, company employees posing as private citizens are most likely promoting legitimate products. If so, you'll have a hard time distinguishing them from the other recommendations. Try to weed out phony or dangerous products and improper presentations. By and large, though, your best bet is to recognize ahead of time that there will be some difficult people, and when they show up, shrug.

VirtualTourist.com

This site, which first appeared in 1999, boasts more than 880,000 registered members and 5 million unique visitors a month. The founders, convinced that the most valuable travel advice comes from other travelers, envisioned a wikinomics-style site where people could share their travel experiences and photographs, and offer tips about local hotels, restaurants, and attractions. That's happened, all right: 1.48 million travel tips on more than 27,000 locations, 2.9 million photos. Forums enable visitors to ask members questions, 85 percent of which are answered. But members have greatly

expanded the nature of the site, sharing information about themselves and making friends. Beyond that, many members have moved VirtualTourist out of the virtual world. They are meeting offline, contributing new content there that eventually finds its way back to the site.

The home page presents a list of so-called travel guides, made up of members' contributions. Each guide is organized under 13 main headings, including "Local Customs" and "Tourist Traps." In Bangkok, along with ads and sponsored links, we found connections to a forum about the city and to discounts on hotels and the like. There was also a list of members, including a Bangkok resident, who had written about the city. Members are encouraged to e-mail contributors for more information.

One of the members who had weighed in on Bangkok— SirRichard, by name—actually lived in Madrid. (His motto: "When in doubt, move.") But he had visited and filed descriptions of 47 countries, ranging from *A* (Albania) to *Z* (Zimbabwe). The general descriptions of his visits might have come from a travel book, but his tips were detailed, personal, and, from the vantage point of other Bangkok visitors, right on target. SirRichard was ranked the fifth most popular contributor on the site, based on the ratings his tips had received from other members.

Fed up with glossy travel publications that too often view destinations through rose-tinted glasses, millions of people now tap into VirtualTourist, and dozens of major companies—from American Airlines to Westin Hotels—are happy to place ads in a virtual environment that deals in realities.

WHAT YOU CAN DO

❖ **Vary content.** It seems obvious now: 1. The public wants honest, dependable information about travel. 2. Travelers love to share their experiences. VirtualTourist simply combined those two facts and created a popular and potentially profitable site. The same equation can work for you, whether you're hoping to crowdsource content for an existing company or for a new company of your own creation. Find something the public wants and needs; present it in such a way that an enthusiastic community will form to meet that demand.

❖ **Vary venues.** Although so much of today's crowdsourcing occurs on the Internet, you should be alert to other venues. The offline meetings of VirtualTourist members are a case in point. Commercial opportunities abound wherever a community exists around an idea or an emotion. The Internet is the most popular medium for marshalling a crowd in your behalf, but it's not the only one.

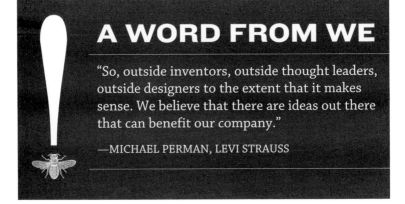

A WORD FROM WE

"So, outside inventors, outside thought leaders, outside designers to the extent that it makes sense. We believe that there are ideas out there that can benefit our company."

—MICHAEL PERMAN, LEVI STRAUSS

ChaCha.com

Even as you read this, somewhere in or above the United States, maybe in a nearby house or the next seat on the plane, a figure sits hunched over a computer, ready and willing to answer any question you might have about anything at any time of the day or night. That's the premise, and the promise, of ChaCha.com, which was founded in December 2005 in Carmel, Indiana, by two impatient entrepreneurs.

ChaCha's chairman and CEO, Scott Jones, invented, at the age of 25, the world's most popular voice mail system (now used by more than 1 billion subscribers). He went on to establish companies in fields as disparate as music-recognition technology and robotics. His innovations show up in Apple's iPod and in robotic lawnmowers. Brad Bostic, ChaCha president, founded Bostech Corporation, which has evolved from custom software development into an enterprise integration software provider; he also built NearMed, a telemedicine service for healthcare providers.

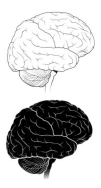

What the two men were impatient about, back in 2005, was traditional search engines. It was taking them too long to sort through the dozens or hundreds of irrelevant answers provided before finding one they were looking for. Their solution was a Web site that combined the investigative talents of machines and the human brain.

A ChaCha search starts when you enter a search term. The instant results are the combination of the best search technology and so-called hand picked sites from the ChaCha community of skilled search experts known as ChaCha guides. If you require further assistance, you can select the option to work directly with a guide. An instant message chat session will begin, and a guide will greet you with a typed message indicating that he or she is ready to help you with your search. Once a guide clarifies what you need, he or she will find the most relevant information and display only those links. If you're not satisfied with your guide's work, you can ask for another.

As of fall 2007, Scott Jones expects to have a community of about 50,000 guides at work, assisting in providing content, and 1 million users of the site. The guides are trained and generally paid between $5 to $10 a search hour—the rate depends upon the reviews they receive from those they help and the number of searches they conduct. The success of the enterprise, all parties agree, will depend on just how good the guides are.

ChaCha searches are free; the
founders hope to make their money
in part, at least, from on-site
advertising. Their serious income,
they say, will come when their
service becomes available to cell
phone users via a toll-free number.

Voice-recognition software will take care of simple searches
such as sport scores, and other searches will be turned over to
the guides. The founders predict that advertisers will be eager
to fill the 15 to 30 seconds when callers are on hold, awaiting
search results.

In case you were wondering, the company's name isn't a
reference to the cha-cha; rather, it comes from the Chinese
word *cha*, which means "search."

Current TV

Viewer-created content, or VC2, makes up about a third
of what's seen on this 24-hour, San Francisco–based,
independent cable and satellite channel—and, not so
incidentally, another non-Internet crowdsourcing venue. The
work makes its way to the television screen by way of a voting
system in which a community of viewers votes on whether
a five-minute piece of film is worthy to be shown on the
airwaves. But getting the green light from viewers still doesn't
guarantee air time; Current TV's producers have the final say
as to which of the viewer-chosen clips are ready for prime
time.

Started by former Vice President Al Gore and entrepreneur
fundraiser Joel Hyatt in August 2005, the channel had a
number of early detractors. *The Wall Street Journal* ridiculed
it, for example, as "newsless, often clueless, and usually dull

WHAT YOU CAN DO

❖ **Maintain quality.** As with many crowdsourced sites, ChaCha has taken steps to keep tabs on its content providers by encouraging customers to rate the guides. (Need we point out that this approach is yet another example of the all-pervasiveness of crowdsourcing? Customers are doing the work that employees handle in traditional organizations.) eBay, for example, has buyers  rating sellers on everything from the speed of delivery to the condition of the item delivered. You have visitors to your site only as long as they're getting the kind of feedback they want, so anything that gets in the way—any failure in the quality of the operation—can easily send them searching elsewhere. Constant vigilance, by employees and/or customers, is the price of profit.

❖ **Go medium rare.** So much of crowdsourcing in this book and elsewhere is mediated by the Internet, which is, in fact, the proximate cause of the whole phenomenon, that ChaCha's telephonic twist is welcome 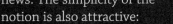 news. The simplicity of the notion is also attractive: No need to fire up the computer or type in search words—just type a few words into the receiver, and your questions get answered. It's as though some Iron Age tool turned out to be a neat substitute for an electronic gadget. The serious message is, look upon every kind of community, on- and offline, as a potential crowdsourcing partner.

... a limp noodle." Based on what's happened in the intervening two years, it turns out that the *Journal* was the clueless one, seriously underestimating the power of wikinomics. Short videos made by up-and-coming filmmakers, citizen reporters, and the viewers themselves are constantly grabbing headlines, and sites such as YouTube, Google Video, and Yahoo! have shown just how popular audience-created entertainment can be.

And Current TV has a couple of very important advantages over these other sites. For one, it has a leg up in ad production. Companies such as Sony, L'Oreal, and Toyota

show commercials made by Current TV viewers, and that typically means a member of the much-sought-after 18-to-34 demographic. So besides getting cut-rate deals on great commercials—L'Oreal paid $1,000 for a stunning and sophisticated viewer-created ad that would have cost it 150 times as much if produced in-house—the advertisers gain insight into the changing tastes of younger consumers.

Second—and, in the long run, maybe even more important—is the distinction between having one's video appear on a Web site and having your work shown on a bona fide television channel. Put another way, it's the difference between a dot-com company and all the baggage that term still carries, and a long-proven business model.

The pieces that make it onto Current TV are a varied palette of trendy cultural items and advocacy journalism that highlights issues such as the ongoing turmoil in the Middle East, poverty in Third World countries, the scourge of AIDs in Africa, and the devastation wrought by Hurricane Katrina. The Katrina piece, shot by a New Orleans resident, aired before network news reporters could even make their way to the city.

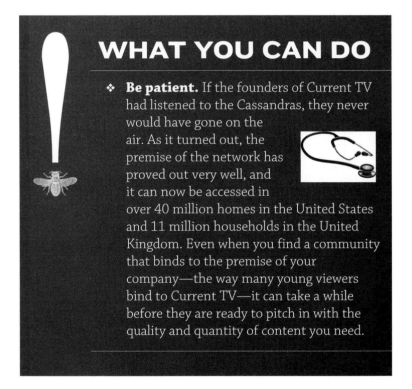

WHAT YOU CAN DO

❖ **Be patient.** If the founders of Current TV had listened to the Cassandras, they never would have gone on the air. As it turned out, the premise of the network has proved out very well, and it can now be accessed in over 40 million homes in the United States and 11 million households in the United Kingdom. Even when you find a community that binds to the premise of your company—the way many young viewers bind to Current TV—it can take a while before they are ready to pitch in with the quality and quantity of content you need.

The essential element that unites all the businesses in this chapter is the willingness—indeed, the eagerness—of the community involved to create product. Year after year, we see improvements in the technology that allows the crowd to produce content. Year after year, we see new online entries that take advantage of the power of community. The opportunities are virtually infinite, limited only by desire and imagination.

In the next chapter, we explore another of crowdsourcing's amazing contributions. Suddenly, there are sites that provide financing for business ventures that might otherwise never get off the ground. Need a loan? Have an idea for a way to tap into the huge cash resources of the crowd? The next chapter is for you.

06

Welcome to the World Bank of We

When Buddy, her cuddly Bichon Frise, hurt his paw, Lyn Townshend of Longmont, Colorado, refused to accept the so-called Elizabethan collar, the uncomfortable plastic cone that makes a dog look as though its head is stuck in a lampshade. So she sewed an elastic strap onto a sock and put the sock on Buddy's paw and the strap around his body, effectively covering the wound and keeping the dog from licking and chewing the dressing. She called it a Strock, combining *strap* and *sock,* and it was a lot more comfortable for the dog—not to mention a lot less attention-getting and embarrassing for its owner.

In fact, it was such a success that Townshend decided she had the makings of a commercial venture. Early in 2006, she formed Best Buddy Pet Products and began turning out designer Strocks on her home sewing machine (www.thestrock.com or www.bestbuddypetproducts.com). The new version was waterproof, came in different sizes to accommodate cats and other noncanine pets, and used adjustable Velcro straps. On just her third sales call, Townshend won the

"The buck doesn't even slow down here."

—ANONYMOUS

endorsement of a veterinary hospital that was part of a 600-strong chain. Suddenly, it looked as though she would have to be ready to produce Strocks by the hundreds—without receiving payment until she delivered the finished goods.

What Townshend needed was a loan. The problem was, she had no income, having quit her job at IBM; she had a record of credit card delinquencies; and she had never run a company. Not surprisingly, she was turned down by her local bank and by the Small Business Administration.

What to do? Wikinomics! Turning to Prosper.com, she joined the community's Business Owners Cooperative, made up of past and would-be borrowers. She posted her loan request on her page at Prosper and would-be lenders bid on it, until finally she was funded by a total of 77 people. On May 21, 2006, she landed a loan of $9,500 at 12.75 percent interest—considerably less than she would have had to pay on a credit card. She used it to buy office equipment, arrange for mass production at a nearby factory, and get her product trademarked.

Prosper is a leading example of the power of community as financier, but it is just the latest twist in the ancient practice of people-to-people lending. Seventeen hundred years ago, long before there were banks or an Internet, there were

communities in China called *lun-hui* whose members helped each other borrow cash. For centuries in the Caribbean, Africa, Korea, and Vietnam, there have been local money pools. Members contribute a set amount each week and take turns picking up the total at the month's end. Known as *susu* in the Caribbean, *kaes* in Korea, and *hui* in Vietnam, these lending societies are common in immigrant communities across the United States. As it happens, that's exactly how Prosper.com came into being.

Back in 1983, Lyna Lam and her family escaped from Vietnam and settled in San Jose, California. They had no income, and all seven of them lived in a studio apartment. Then they joined their neighbors, pooling what money they could scrape together in a *hui*. They used it to buy a car and, eventually, start a landscaping business.

Meanwhile, Chris Larsen was graduating from San Francisco State University with a degree in accounting. After spending a few years working for Chevron, he earned an MBA at Stanford and, in 1992, started a mortgage business. Four years later, he launched E-Loan, which closed more than $27 billion in consumer loans before he sold it to Popular Inc. in 2005 for $300 million. For his next act, Larsen established Prosper.com.

Where did he get the idea? Partially from his wife, Lyna Lam. As she told *Business Week,* "He was fascinated by how [the Vietnamese] work together and come through for each other."

The basic advantages of borrowing and lending on these sites are clear and simple: Borrowers pay less interest than they would otherwise; lenders get better returns.

Prosper came online in February 2006. It works very much like eBay, except that what is being auctioned is a loan, not a used bicycle or a collection of comic books. Registration is free. Borrowers get a page on the site to list the size of the loan they want—the upper limit is $25,000—and the interest rate they're willing to pay. They also present their reason for the loan and as much information about themselves as they think will help attract lenders. Prosper runs credit checks on potential borrowers, assigning them one of eight scores, from AA (the top rating) to HR ("High Risk"), to NC ("No Credit History"). It also provides the borrower's debt-to-income ratio. The auction can last from three to seven days, at the borrower's discretion.

Prosper encourages borrowers to join one of the thousands of groups that have formed around a single leader and generally consist of people who have something in common, whether service in the armed forces, or a degree from Penn State, or a divorce. By joining a group whose members have achieved a successful record of repaying loans, the borrower can attract more offers from lenders at lower rates because the group as a whole carries less risk of delinquency. The group leader provides guidance, but it can come at a price: The leader  can collect a reward of up to $20 when a member's loan gets funded—and another bonus each time a borrower makes a monthly payment on time. Many don't take these "shared rewards," though.

Because the groups function as separate communities within the larger community on the site, they exert a degree of discipline on their members. Like the members of a *hui*, group members fear losing face if they miss their payments. They are also aware that such behavior tarnishes the group's  record, with financial consequences for all its would-be borrowers.

Successful borrowers pay Prosper a 1 to 2 percent fee when a loan comes through, while registered lenders pay a 0.5 to 1 percent annual servicing fee on their outstanding loans. Just over a year after its founding, the company had marked up 11,100 loans totaling more than $65 million. Approximately 2 percent of funded loans in dollar terms or 3 percent (339 loans) of funded loans in unit terms have defaulted.

A WORD FROM WE

"Exotic though this may sound, a recent study found that three quarters of consumers would consider borrowing online through a social lending community."

—GROUP CONTRIBUTION

Zopa

Before there was Prosper.com, there was Zopa, established in spring 2005. Where Prosper presents itself in sober, bankerly fashion, Zopa has a chip on its shoulders

toward banks and other stick-in-the-muds. "Whatever you call [us]," its Web site pleads, "please don't call us a bank." "Marketplace" is preferred. What's so bad about banks? They have "huge overheads, with thousands of employees to pay, hundreds of branches to *feng shui,* and countless fat cats to feed. And they take more than their fair share of people's money."

There are substantive differences as well between the two social-lending sites, as they're known. Zopa does not rely on separate communities of members to improve borrowers' chances and diminish lenders' risks. Would-be borrowers are put through credit checks and a risk-assessment process; those who pass receive a rating from A* to C, depending on their risk profile. Zopa offers borrowers a protection policy that keeps those monthly repayment checks going in case of illness, accident, or loss of job.

Lenders announce the rate of return they seek, what level A* to C they want to lend to, and when they want their money back. Their loans are then divided into small chunks and distributed among potential borrowers. There must be at least 50 lenders for every loan of 500 pounds or more, and no one is allowed to borrow twice from the same person. Lenders receive 4.5 percent interest on their funds that have not yet been lent out.

As of the spring of 2007, *The Daily Telegraph* reported, Zopa listed 135,000 members and an average annual return to lenders of 6.8 percent. More than half of those applying for Zopa loans flunk their credit checks and are turned down. Something like 1 percent of A-rated borrowers are in default, and that rises to 3 percent for C-rated borrowers.

In at least one department, Zopa is unashamed to compare itself to banks: "A collections agency chases any missed payments on each lender's behalf. This is exactly the same process that banks and other financial institutions use." Of course, unlike banks, Zopa's loans are not covered by Britain's Financial Services Compensation Scheme—nor by America's Federal Deposit Insurance Corporation, for that matter.

Yes, Zopa has launched itself into the
U.S. market with a base in San Francisco
and $15 million from Bessemer Venture
Partners, America's oldest venture
capital firm. "We can assure you, it will
be a distinctly American cake," the company promised, "more
of a brownie than a scone, if you like."

WHAT YOU CAN DO

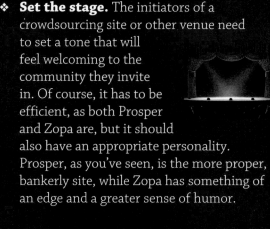

- ❖ **Set the stage.** The initiators of a
  crowdsourcing site or other venue need
  to set a tone that will
  feel welcoming to the
  community they invite
  in. Of course, it has to be
  efficient, as both Prosper
  and Zopa are, but it should
  also have an appropriate personality.
  Prosper, as you've seen, is the more proper,
  bankerly site, while Zopa has something of
  an edge and a greater sense of humor.

- ❖ **Go the extra mile.** It's almost as though
  the creators of Zopa sat down, having put
  the basic lending and borrowing procedures
  in place, and said to
  themselves, "What else can
  we do to make members
  feel comfortable?" And
  they found things, too.
  On the lenders' side, it was the decision to
  pay decent interest on unlent loan money.
  On the borrowers' side, it was the offering
  of insurance against accident or job loss. It
  only makes sense.

A WORD FROM WE

"Microlending Web sites provide the ability for individuals to lend to small businesses directly. The underwriting decisions (assessing the risk of each loan) are made by individuals, and the price of a loan is established through lender bidding. We expect these lending decisions to be superior to the same decisions currently made by experts at banks."

—REX MILLER, MEMBER OF THE WE ARE SMARTER COMMUNITY

CommonAngels

In June 1998, in a restaurant not far from the Boston Common, a handful of former software company CEOs sat down around a breakfast table and created something new in the world. As private investors, they had individually provided funds to support start-ups. They now agreed to become a community of angels, jointly considering, selecting, and financing high-potential, early-stage information technology companies. They decided to call their firm CommonAngels, in honor of those nearby historic meeting grounds.

Since then, this experiment in crowdsourcing has succeeded beyond its founders' dreams. Its membership has grown to 70 investors plus five dozen limited partners in two coinvestment funds. It has collectively funded 34 companies with $38 million and has had numerous successes. And it has inspired dozens of other groups of angel investors to follow suit.

In many ways, CommonAngels demonstrates the power inherent in community, not just in the finance area, but in every aspect of business. Because of the firm's communal nature, its members—seasoned entrepreneurs with expertise in software, IT, and the Internet—bring the sum of their knowledge and experience to every investment decision. They also bring their thousands of personal and professional relationships to bear, providing a strong flow of deals and relevant expertise. And because their own money is riding on it, they're seriously involved in the process.

An angel community is quite unlike a traditional venture capital (VC) operation. VC firms usually invest other people's money, based upon the judgment of managers who are paid a fee and a share of the profits, and face little or no downside risk. The members of the angel group win all or lose all. It makes for a very different decision-making process—and a very different investment profile.

According to James Geshwiler, a founder and a managing director of CommonAngels, a major benefit of the communal approach is that it can't be gamed. When a VC committee of three or four people sits down to vote on funding projects, each of the members is likely to have a favorite; to get his or her project approved by the others, a member will hedge his or her critique of their projects. The committee decisions also depend on the relationships among the members—who's up or down, who wants to impress whom. A clever start-up CEO can play to that audience.

"At CommonAngels, we get 40 people in a room," Geshwiler says. "That's too many to game. And they're all voting their own checkbook. So what do I care what you think about what I think? I only care about what you think about the company under consideration. I'm not going to hold back what I really think, and neither are you. We're going to draw each other out."

A start-up seeking support begins by e-mailing the angel group its business plan's executive summary. Geshwiler e-mails copies of the summary to a few members who are knowledgeable about the company's project area. If they're enthusiastic, the start-up's leader is invited to make a presentation to those members and another two or three

who are what Geshwiler calls "generalists." Specialists can become "victims of their own experience and make assumptions," he says. "Generalists ask the basic questions, such as 'Why is this such a good idea?'" Too often, he adds, an investor acting individually makes his or her decisions on the basis of only one or two risks, while failing to test more rigorously basic questions, such as: What are the fundamental dynamics of the market for the product? Or, how hard is it really to make the technology work? If the start-up passes muster at that level, its leader moves on to the final stage: a presentation before 40 or more members.

At every stage, the questions fly and the members discuss and debate the various issues with the start-up leader and with each other. Sometimes when an entrepreneur describes how he wants to build his company, Geshwiler says, "It's like watching the Red Sea part: the ex-Microsoft people on one side, the ex-Lotus people on the other, and a 20-year-old argument comes back—centralized architecture versus distributed systems."

Because of the checks and balances built into the community approach, CommonAngels reaches a consensus that is far more often right than wrong. But none of it is easy. Geshwiler offers an example of a start-up called Skyhook Wireless,

whose product, a virtual GPS, was capable of correcting the problem GPS has in big cities because the tall buildings block the line of sight to the satellite. The company said its invention could be used to fix GPS in automotive navigation systems, wi-fi cell phones, and other devices. The angel group "debated and debated" over which, if any, of the applications represented a substantial market, and finally decided to invest $1.5 million. Sure enough, the start-up has signed a major deal to have its product embedded in a GPS chip.

CommonAngels has developed techniques to avoid some of the potential pitfalls of group decision making—the bandwagon effect, for example, when members rush to join an acknowledged expert after he offers an early review of a company. After a presentation, the large group is divided into separate tables of five or six people. Each table elects a reporter who summarizes the table's conclusions for the larger group. During the discussion, members are expected to fill out and hand in so-called evaluation sheets indicating their attitude toward the proposed investment. The goal is to ensure that the members are exposed to all the arguments, pro and con, and are given ample opportunity to make their own feelings known.

The community's decisions, Geshwiler says, are based upon assumptions about a company, including the abilities and integrity of its leaders and the market for its products. After an initial investment, CommonAngels insists on testing its assumptions. It sends teams of members on follow-up visits to the company, usually on a six-month schedule. Once again, he explains, the numbers matter. When a VC firm's partner who championed an investment in a company pays a follow-up visit, that person is looking for good news because his or her reputation in the firm is on the line. CommonAngels members have no such concern. And with a whole team of people, Geshwiler adds, the company's leader has far less chance to hide his or her situation: "There's a lot more incentive to just get everything out on the table." That comes in handy when it's time to think about a follow-up round of investing.

WHAT YOU CAN DO

❖ **Expertise is not everything.** As a community dedicated to making the right decision, CommonAngels recognized from the get-go that it needed a broad range of expertise in its chosen area of information technology. So it made sure its membership list included people with a wide variety of skills. At the same time, the firm brought in people whose entrepreneurial experience was outside technology—generalists who could look at a proposed deal from a larger, nontechnical perspective. Communities need both kinds of members.

❖ **Turn the discussion on its head.** From a sponsor's point of view, decision making in a community is fraught with potential problems—it's all too susceptible to all sorts of negative, ill-advised influences. A small group can easily lead the larger community down a path to a disastrous conclusion. A single charismatic individual can turn a discussion on its head. Personal agendas and personality conflicts can create havoc. What's needed are people, like CommonAngels' leaders, who have an understanding of group dynamics and can develop procedures to guard against such problems.

There's a wide divide between Prosper and Zopa, on the one hand, and CommonAngels, on the other—between Lyn Townshend's $9,500 loan to make Strocks and a million-dollar investment in a high-tech start-up. What we have tried to suggest is the close to infinite variety of ways in which communities can be used to perform a company's finance function. Approaches might vary, but in all cases, the focus is on finding ways to minimize the lender's risk by providing the maximum amount of relevant information.

The next chapter discusses the role crowdsourcing might play in actually managing an organization. Is such a thing possible? Turn the page, and you'll find out.

07

Make Everyone a C-We-O

Up to this point in the book, we have deluged you with successful examples of crowdsourcing at work—communities of individuals cheerfully performing virtually every business function, from product design to finance. This chapter is different because we have arrived at the activity that cuts across all functions: management. Here our central question is: Can a community successfully determine the direction of a company, making strategic decisions about what products or services to pursue and how to create, market, and distribute them?

The answer, to date, has been no—and not for lack of trying. Perhaps the most thorough and intensive effort so far was undertaken in June 2005 by Rob May, an engineer, an entrepreneur, and founder of Businesspundit.com. He established a project called TheBusinessExperiment.com (TBE), which quickly attracted more than 800 members, all of them eager to participate in what promised to be a historic, groundbreaking venture. Together members selected a product—another Web site—and it was eventually designed and launched. Sad to say, in March 2006, just nine months after its birth, TBE was voted out of existence.

"If things seem under control, you're not going fast enough."

—MARIO ANDRETTI

In a pointed essay on Businesspundit.com, May offered his explanation for the failure of his experiment. "The wisdom of crowds is huge right now," he wrote. "Old businesses are dead. It's all about  embracing edge competencies and network effects. ... I don't buy it. Business is still business."

Yes, we agree, business is still business, but we beg to differ with his other conclusions. There is simply too much evidence of the successful leveraging of communities—successful in traditional business terms—to write off the power of we. At the same time, a number of vital lessons can be learned from the short but fascinating TBE experience, particularly as it pertains to the ability of a community to manage and lead an organization.

The initial TBE Web site was envisioned as an incubator for a fully transparent exercise in P2P, or peer-to-peer, creativity. On it, visitors would become members; via discussion

 forums, members would talk about their plans, make decisions, and read progress reports. Their only reward, aside from personal satisfaction in helping the site move ahead, would be points based upon a member's contributions to the project. Point totals would determine what share of the hoped-for profits a member received.

During TBE's first weeks, members submitted some 60 ideas for new businesses, which were debated in the forums and

then voted on in serial fashion. Finalists included a social-networking site for business travelers and a kiosk for selling MP3 files. In the end, members chose to create Askspace.com, which would tap the wisdom of members to provide solutions to problems small business owners presented.

Because members received equity, TBE had to file a private placement offering early on, and the legal costs were considerable. May had assumed that "someone with more money than sense" would "throw

$25K" at the project, enabling it to pay legal bills and even outsource some of the technical work. It never happened. As a result, if Askspace was to succeed, the members would have to make it happen themselves.

A WORD FROM WE

"These folks sustained Apple by supporting its customers when Apple couldn't—or didn't want to—support them itself. Now that Apple is the homecoming queen again, there are lots of people receiving, taking, and claiming credit for its success. The Apple user-group community deserves a high-five tribute, too."

—GUY KAWASAKI, VENTURE CAPITALIST AND
  FORMER APPLE FELLOW

When the final venture was settled upon, though, many members lost interest, presumably because the ideas they favored had lost out. A third of them never logged onto TBE again. Only about 200 members remained actively committed, and a mere 30 of them joined four leadership teams. In October, member David Gibbons wrote on the site, "Organizing these groups functionally has been a challenge, mostly to the democracy that made TBE so appealing in the first place."

It had become evident that top-down leadership was needed, and TBE member Sean Clauson, a database programmer from Minneapolis, Minnesota, volunteered to become chief

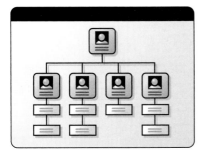

executive officer. As Rob May put it, "Sean built a leadership team and really drove the project forward." The five members of that team met for the first time in October, via Skype, and talked for two hours.

High on their list of topics was the membership's remarkable enthusiasm for Gibbons's proposal to split the new venture into a large number of small tasks and allow members to choose which they would take on, an approach known as microchunking. More than 91 percent of the community endorsed the plan, as compared to an average 41 percent approval for the previous six proposals, including the Askspace name.

As it turned out, though, members were
better at voting than working. "We
had an abundance of expert opinion,"
Gibbons wrote in March, "but those same
experts' time is in very short supply, so
getting actual work done became almost
impossible." Nevertheless, a beta version
of Askspace was launched.

Soon afterward, Rob May wrote, "We came to realize that
the way we operated was no different from other companies.
Decisions were made at high levels because there wasn't
time to put everything up to a vote to the crowd. In addition,
the crowd sometimes voted in ways that gave us conflicting
direction." When he put Askspace's future to a vote, the nays
won.

May offered several lessons TBE had taught him. For
example, having members vote on which business idea to
pursue was the wrong approach. He should have started with
a new business clearly in mind. Then, he wrote, "I would have
attracted the right people—people that liked that particular
idea. Instead, I attracted people that primarily liked to discuss
ideas."

To gain members' wholehearted support, May maintained,
a P2P business must tailor its incentives to their
tastes. TBE's members were "a successful bunch,"
he explained, and, as a consequence, they were
short on time. Even 30 minutes a week turned
out to be too much. What was needed was a truly
involved and committed membership that would be
satisfied by the intangible incentives of "knowledge,
satisfaction of their curiosity, and the desire to
succeed."

In the beginning, May had hoped the membership would be self-directed. He became convinced that this was an expectation not grounded in reality. Large groups, he wrote, need leaders who understand not only the whole project, but the context of all individual aspects of the project: "If everybody has an equal voice, it can lead to lots of talking in circles and very little productive decision making." At least, that's what happened at TBE.

Meanwhile, Askspace has an afterlife in the form of a site called Askspace.blogspot.com. It was established by Carolyn Burke, one of the first five leaders of TBE. (She is also generally accorded the honor of having invented the blog when she put her personal diary online in 1995.) Her latest site is described as "a metablog about Askspace's principles: wisdom of crowds, transparency, business ownership, Web 2.0."

A WORD FROM WE

"Wikipedia [has] bureaucrats, stewards, and administrators. These roles are formed either by election or promotion, and they possess blanket edit, deletion, or account revocation rights. The point to be made here is that intrinsic within the nature of self-governance of the Wikipedia is the presence of roles for monitoring and control, albeit democratic."

—CHANDRIKA SAMARTH, MEMBER OF THE WE ARE SMARTER COMMUNITY

In the first chapter of this book, we briefly discussed another effort to use crowdsourcing to perform a variety of roles, including that of management. Cambrian House relies on a community of 30,000 individuals to come up with new ideas, try them out, suggest improvements, and then connect with other interested members to build and commercialize it. Points toward a share of any eventual profit and cash up front are awarded to idea inventors and those who spend time adding or improving features. As of spring 2007, all four of the company's underwritten crowdsourced products were proceeding on course, with more than 200 other ideas under development by the Cambrian House community without any interference from the company itself.

cambrianhouse
home of crowdsourcing

So here we have a successful example of a community taking on some managerial duties, although there needs to be an asterisk beside that sentence. In the TBE project, the attempt was made to enlist the community in actually developing a chosen product—an attempt that eventually failed. At Cambrian, employees perform and manage some tasks (designing, manufacturing, and the like) if the company invests in or works directly with a community member's project.

Suffice it to say, then, that our two examples at least leave the door open to the possibility that communities will eventually be able to handle substantial management tasks. We're on much firmer ground, though, with the other business functions that the "power of we" taps.

08

Lead from the Rear

All through history, leaders have sought to persuade or compel communities to change their ways. The more drastic the change desired, the less likely the success. The "Great Leap Forward" of China's Communist leader Mao Zedong, for example, imposed a whole new political structure on his people in his rush to industrialize. It was a major disaster: Millions died of starvation, and the economy was devastated. Fifty years later, Mao's folly remains a cautionary tale for anyone who hopes to control the attitudes and actions of a group of independent people.

毛泽东 1893-

As we have argued throughout this book, wikinomic communities can often perform real-world tasks faster,

better, and cheaper than individuals. But building a successful community is no simple matter. Here, as in all aspects of business, from hiring to marketing, the price of great rewards is great risk. And that has never been so true as in the era of Web 2.0, when a seemingly minor mistake can snowball into a fatal disaster with lightning speed.

"I must follow the people. Am I not their leader?"

—BENJAMIN DISRAELI, BRITISH STATESMAN

This chapter lays out a series of guidelines intended to help companies avoid some of the pitfalls along the 2.0 road. They reflect the experience of leaders who have followed that crowdsourcing route—men and women who have shared their trials and triumphs on www.wearesmarter.org, the online community we established on the way to writing this book.

I. Lead from the Rear

It takes a company a lot of time, money, and effort to build a community. Inevitably, the temptation arises to run it like any other part of the enterprise. That's a bad idea. The whole point of crowdsourcing is to access the fresh, powerful ideas and instincts of the community. The company's role is to provide direction and then stand back: Interference with communal processes defeats the purpose.

In other words, the company is not the star of the show, but the producer, working from behind the scenes to make it

easy and comfortable for all community members to get involved and stay involved. The words and ideas should be allowed to flow unimpeded: a collective stream of consciousness. When overzealous managers interrupt and derail the conversation, valuable ideas are lost.

As we mentioned at the start of the book, when Jeff Bezos opened Amazon's database to savvy outsiders, he didn't tell them what to do with it. He announced, "We're going to aggressively expose ourselves!" He left it to the crowd to figure out how best to use the site, and he profited mightily.

2. Know When to Step In

Communities have built-in self-correcting capacities. Troublemakers get squelched or ignored; bad information gets corrected. On craigslist.org, for instance, whenever an ad breaks the site's terms of service—say, a seemingly personal appeal turns out to be a link to a Web site—or if a post is miscategorized or is really spam, the community members are all over it like a terrier chasing a cat. More than 25 percent of craigslist postings are flagged for removal by members, and of that number, an amazing 95 percent turn out to be violations.

Still, the threats to community operations are endless and often ingenious. Sometimes they come from those who have a special agenda in mind for the group—an outside marketer, say, who's hoping to capitalize on a group's size to peddle his or her own company's products or even hijack the community

to do his or her selling. Sometimes the threats are simply the work of twisted minds—so-called flamers, for example, who seek to entertain themselves by creating trouble. They like to post a controversial, hostile message on a community's site for the sole purpose of stirring up an angry response and a disruptive debate. Or the troublemaker could be a hacker, like the one we talked about in Chapter 3, "How May We Help We?", who wreaked havoc

in Chapter 3, "How May We Help We?", who wreaked havoc with PMI Audio's community forums.

When flamers or other intruders hinder a community's operations and remain unchecked, the company should not hesitate to step in. By the same token, if the misinformation being bandied about might cause someone to make a potentially harmful or costly mistake, managers owe it to the community—and to the company—to clarify ASAP. In all cases, though, such intrusions should be brief and hedged with explanations.

That same caveat applies to those moments when the community seems a tad too messy or even drifting toward chaos. Let's face it, people want to type in their own favorite

fonts, punctuate any way that suits them, and express themselves in idiosyncratic ways. Just like the folks who man the Cookshack forums back in Chapter 3, they also will tell off-color stories, brag about their grandchildren,

and generally wander off-topic. All this is understandable and even beneficial in principle: Original ideas often emerge from such spontaneous, off-the-cuff behavior. Communities thrive on the unexpected and the spontaneous.

But if communities wander too far from their mission for too long, company managers need to find ways to weigh in— summarizing the discussion, for example, to move it forward.

It can be tricky to maintain an unfettered environment that encourages original thinking yet never gets so tumultuous or off-point that it fails to function properly. Best to err on the side of *laissez-faire*. Otherwise, you'll never know how many groundbreaking concepts and comments your community was deprived of hearing.

And if you're relying on community members to perform a service function, consider following the path of companies such as ChaCha.com and eBay that ask customers to rate the service help they've been given.

3. Form a Club, a Real Community of Like-Minded People

Creating a vibrant community is all about creating a critical mass of good minds and spurring them to spark off each other. But the odds of success improve when the members share the same general outlook—it simply makes it easier for them to communicate and cooperate. Their energy is spent on the company's mission, not on quarreling over their differences. A mix of jocks and nerds, say, or left-wingers and right-wingers, is less likely to achieve the trust and commitment needed to evoke and maximize the group's collective knowledge. That thought must have weighed heavily with Virgin Mobile USA managers when they sifted through their list of online customers to create their 2,000-member "insiders" community, the one we talked about in Chapter 2, "Go from R&D to R&We."

A company's first target group in forming a community should be those who have a clear interest in connecting with

the organization—satisfied customers, for example, or residents of towns where the company operates. The secondary goal is to enroll as many bright people

CREATING A VIBRANT COMMUNITY IS ALL ABOUT
CREATING A CRITICAL MASS OF GOOD MINDS AND
SPURRING THEM TO SPARK OFF EACH OTHER.

as possible. An exciting circle of like-minded people can be a magnet for others at a time when business needs all the good minds it can find.

Success today depends on amassing intellectual property, strengthening brands, and holding on to fickle customers, all of which require very smart people. They're in short supply, partly because of the newly global talent hunt and partly because talented people can pick and choose where they settle and dictate their own terms.

The bright people needed to create a vibrant community are likely to be so involved in the conversation that they carry it on beyond the virtual venue. Encourage them to do so, to keep talking and thinking about the community wherever they are. Suggest that they work the room at conferences and exchange phone calls, e-mail, and snail mail—anything to help members uncover shared interests, strengthen connections, and deepen personal bonds. Remember those offline meetings sponsored by the VirtualTourist community? The object of all such activities: a cohesive community that grows ideas with all the bursting vitality of a cornfield in July.

Size matters, too. The community must be large and smart enough to ride herd on the content it produces, catching and correcting mistakes and improper additions as they occur.

Generally, the bigger the collective brain, the greater the variety of viewpoints and information, and the better the content. As the members interact, they absorb one another's interests and expand their horizons so that what might have begun as a community focused on marketing, for instance, gradually branches out to innovate in other processes vital to its corporate sponsor.

4. You Can't Hide, So Don't Even Try

It's an inescapable truth of this transparent age that sooner or later—and, mostly, sooner—the errors a company commits will be exposed for everyone to see. When a mistake is made in working with a community, the best course is to admit it without delay, apologize, and make sure it's not repeated.

When an error surfaces, there's a natural inclination to hunker down and hope it will all go away. Companies put off responding—or, worse yet, erase e-mails and otherwise try to deny or pretend that nothing happened. Not a good idea. As we've seen "on the highest levels," cover-ups have a way of making matters worse.

The same goes for the tired old art of spinning, the biased and deceptive effort to put the best face on an unfavorable incident. Spin destroys the implied covenant a company has with its community and can create all sorts of havoc.

Take a lesson from CBS News. In spring 2007, in one of her "Notebook" segments on the company Web site, Katie Couric presented a piece that began "I still remember when I first got my library card." The problem, as the network learned too late, was that the rest of the piece had actually been written by a CBS producer—and the producer, in turn, had actually stolen large chunks of it from an article in *The Wall Street Journal.* CBS quickly went public with the story, replacing the piece with a "correction" and firing the offending producer. The network also explained that the ghostwriting of anchors' commentary was a routine practice ("That's the way television generally works," a spokeswoman said. "It's a very collaborative medium.") and that Couric did write some of her pieces.

There was a predictable uproar that took some time to settle down, partly because of Couric's high-profile, big-money debut as the first female evening-news anchor and her subsequent poor showing in the ratings. But CBS was able to contain the damage by its decision to go public with the error and its willingness to explain the process used to prepare the "Notebook" segments.

The bottom line is this: In a world where the inner workings of government and business are daily revealed through e-mails, companies need to erase the word *confidential* from their mental hard drives. The whistleblowers reign supreme, abetted by those ever-more-powerful online search engines whose algorithms don't distinguish between good news and bad.

So if a company's reputation with its community is tarnished by some misstep, denials and evasions are the wrong way to go. The company needs to 'fess up, explain how it happened, and transgress no more. (P.S. It might also find some creative ways to let the community know about the positive things the company has accomplished lately.)

5. Forget about Perfection

Anything that gets members of a
community talking is good. Anything that
slows that conversation is bad. When a
company communication is too flashy or
too finely tuned, it can rapidly shut down
discussion and make it impossible to get the
valuable feedback the company seeks.

We all experience the phenomenon in our
daily lives. We're sitting with friends or
family around the kitchen table or at the
neighborhood bar, the banter and easy talk

bouncing back and forth, when
a newcomer joins in. There's
nothing really wrong with
him—he's pleasant and articulate, offering
very intelligent, cogent opinions and ideas—
but somehow his presence is an intrusion. The
jokes fall flat. The flights of fancy are grounded.

That's more or less what happens when companies' messages
are too perfect, too polished. Overly explained and edited
topical material makes people feel as if everything has already
been said, thus deterring them from jumping in with their
own observations and opinions. Instead, many companies
adopt a comfortable, down-home tone, and some even
sprinkle their remarks with grammatical or spelling errors.
The object is to give the company a human face and avoid
language that might be seen as officious or patronizing.

Southwest Airlines, long admired as the master of the
discounters, is also a master at communicating with its
communities. Its "Nuts About Southwest" blog, for example,

is written by different employees each month but is open to customers and the public as well. They weigh in with comments and complaints. That's why the company likens the blog to an "online watercooler." The blogs and the comments are all part of a comfortable, easygoing conversation that ensures the company of an interested, involved community of employees and customers.

Just how involved was made clear in 2006 when a blog by CEO Gary Kelly reported that the company might change its, if you will, long-standing open-seating policy. Hundreds of customers and employees complained at the prospect of being told where to sit. As they made clear, Southwest's unique first-come seating policy had been one reason customers kept coming back. Open seating was saved. By starting an unscripted conversation with customers, Southwest got some invaluable firsthand feedback from the people who foot its bills and pay its employees' salaries.

The tidy perfection of polished presentations is the wrong tack to take with a community.

6. Stir Things Up

There's nothing quite so blah and unproductive as a homogeneous, complacent community Web site. The sponsoring company is looking for new ideas, instructive feedback, and a glimpse of future customer trends. Instead, it sees nothing but platitudes and familiar comments—many of them favorable, to be sure, but none of them truly helpful. It's time for the company to step in and stir things up.

What's needed is a real debating club, one in which all viewpoints on a particular topic are welcome. Companies need to make sure that contrary opinions are encouraged, that members start challenging the revealed wisdoms of the group. It's in the play of argument and counterargument that fresh ideas rise to the surface.

Glenn Kelman, CEO of the online real estate brokerage firm Redfin, embraced contrariness with a passion when he decided to "tell all" online and allow his competitors to savage him in plain sight of customers.

As recounted by Clive Thompson in the April 2007 issue of *Wired* magazine, Kelman raised the hackles of old-line real estate agents when he sliced commissions for sellers to about a third of the typical rate. His rivals retaliated by refusing to sell houses to anyone who used Redfin's service.

Kelman suffered in silence for months. Then he took to blogging. But he also shined the hot light of publicity on his competitors' greedy practices, while allowing them to freely state their cases via comments on the company's Web site. They let fly with nasty comments, and Kelman returned fire with his own zingers.

Potential homebuyers loved tuning in for the next episode in the battle of the brokers, and that began to make Kelman's

enemies nervous. They realized that airing their industry's dirty laundry in public might not be good for anyone's business, but they were only partially right.

Redfin's revenues were growing. By presenting both sides of the debate and being honest about his own mistakes and problems, he had created an online community of sympathetic would-be customers.

The goal is to create a site that touches people where they live, that elicits involvement and passion—and that means finding the right proposition. One example we pointed to was Zebo. com, whose success is based on the fact that young people are passionate about what they own and want to own.

7. Say Thank You

Companies that sponsor communities need to remember that a transaction is taking place. The members of the communities are sharing themselves and their talents in ways that have value for the companies, and their contributions deserve to be acknowledged and rewarded.

Gather.com, for instance, uses a point system to reward member participation. The more its members join in the discussion, the more points they earn for spending on goods and services provided by Gather's partners. People who frequently contribute quality content to the site can even earn cash rewards.

As indicated in earlier chapters, different companies take different approaches. Some, such as P&G, keep active community members in the loop with news about upcoming products and samples of the same. Others, such as InnoCentive, hold out the possibility of making thousands of dollars if a community member can solve a scientific problem. Whatever approach a company plans to take to thank its community, the community should first review it to make sure it is perceived as fair and adequate. Anything less will defeat the purpose and leave the members frustrated and annoyed.

Many communities, such as Gather.com, reward their top contributors, but not everyone has equal access to a computer, and many people have a lifestyle that permits only infrequent contributions. Moreover, one provocative or brilliant post can outweigh a string of mundane comments. It's important for companies to remember those members whose value is very real but cannot be easily measured by number of contributions.

8. This Is Not a One-Night Stand

Communities take time to develop. Attracting a cast of valuable characters who share common interests cannot be accomplished overnight, and establishing and strengthening the personal relationships so necessary to a productive environment is a long-term proposition. This should not be rushed. You might remember our description of Current TV, the station Al Gore helped create, which critics wrote off after a slow start; it's doing just fine now, thank you very much.

While the community is forming, companies need to experiment with content and ways of inciting valuable discussion. Community members themselves should be enlisted in that process, providing feedback and their own suggestions for keeping the idea pot bubbling. At the same time, companies would do well to help members improve their collaborative abilities, perhaps by encouraging them to get involved in other collaborative environments.

Above all, sponsors should pay attention, observing the interactions and flow of ideas within their communities and monitoring community reactions to the sponsors' initiatives. Sponsors need to develop their own sets of goals for their communities and to establish target dates for the evaluation of their virtual ventures. For a new group, a year or 18 months is soon enough to make a determination of whether the game has been worth the candle.

At the start of this book, we described the revolutionary impact that communities are having on the way business is conducted—their ability to devise new products and services, provide customer service, improve sales and manufacturing, and tap into new sources of financing. We also promised to help you better understand how to make that happen in your own company by organizing, inspiring, and maintaining your own community. As we reach the end of our journey together, we sincerely hope that we have lived up to that promise.

But whatever your feelings are about this book, we urge you to continue your exploration of the crowdsourcing phenomenon. It is the wave of the future, and you should be riding it.

Speaking of the future, in the pages just ahead, we offer a short afterword about the tremendous transformation that is taking place in the nature of work, including the relationship between companies and their employees. You'll not be surprised, we suspect, to find that we—and large numbers of experts—believe that communities of workers will have a starring role.

Afterword—Join the Crowd

In his 1990 hit play *Six Degrees of Separation*, John Guare has one of his characters say, "I read somewhere that everybody on this planet is separated by only six other people.

... The President of the United States, a gondolier in Venice, just fill in the names. I find it extremely comforting that we're so close."

That six-degree equation evolved from the 1967 experiment of a social psychologist named Stanley Milgram, who had volunteers mail packages to 100 people at random. Columbia University professors repeated the experiment in 2002, but this time it was via e-mail, and some 60,000 people from 166 nations participated. The result, though, was pretty much the same. An average of no more than six links separated one e-mailer from another. Whether you find that comforting, though, is another matter.

The world as we've known it is changing all around us, and a big part of that change is in the nature of the connections between people and between people and their employers. Computers, cell phones, iPods, and the Internet are making us more distinctly individual and independent. We spend more time away from the office, working and traveling, and a great deal more time online, accessing information for our work and communicating with colleagues, suppliers, and customers. Although the Internet has made workers more independent, it has also led them to create communities built upon collaboration. In other words, our degree of separation from our customary work life has increased, while, at the same time, we have never been so widely connected.

Experts such as Gartner Inc., a Connecticut-based technology research and advisory company, expect that these developments will drastically alter the nature of work over the next decade. Freed from dependence upon the company for infrastructure and resources, employees will provide intangible services from their own personally customized workspaces. They will rely on networks of people, many of them unaffiliated with their employer, for advice, information, and best practices.

Inevitably, their relationship to the company will be transformed. The expertise they have chosen and developed will allow them to move easily from one employer to another, erasing whatever vestiges of company loyalty remain. They will insist that collaboration, much of it remote, replace the traditional authoritarian interactions of manager and employee. As Gartner put it in a recent report, the new relationship will be one of symbiosis. Indeed, we believe that the corporation as it now exists, with its armies of salaried workers in identical cubicles, will gradually disappear. Instead, there will be virtual communities that will be able to mobilize teams of specialists to take on necessary tasks for customers.

FREED FROM DEPENDENCE UPON THE COMPANY FOR INFRASTRUCTURE AND RESOURCES, EMPLOYEES WILL PROVIDE INTANGIBLE SERVICES FROM THEIR OWN PERSONALLY CUSTOMIZED WORKSPACES.

How rapidly is the U.S. moving toward a virtual life? According to the Kaiser Family Foundation, between 1999 and 2004, children's time on the computer doubled, along with huge increases in their hours spent in chat rooms, interactive channels, and instant messaging. When they grow up, online connectedness will seem like the obvious option for play or work.

For now, though, the work changes we have discussed are still early days—companies have plenty of time to prepare to meet them. Leaders need to examine their management and support policies, and adjust them to fit the more collaborative model

their newly independent employees seek. A policy carved in stone simply doesn't suffice for the new-breed workers who thrive on challenge and are constantly seeking out-of-the-box assignments that will boost their expertise. At the same time, companies should become knowledgeable about the care and feeding of virtual networks and communities, which play such an important role in the work life of the newly independent worker.

One way to get started is to join us on our Web site, **www.wearesmarter.org**.

You might recall that we introduced the site back in the introduction to this book. We had hoped the members would actually write the book for us. That did not happen, but they have continued to offer their insights, sharing their experiences and best practices with other members.

We hope the readers of this book will join our community, not only to benefit from the posts of other members and from the occasional in-person meetings, but to share with us their own stories. That seems to us the best of all possible worlds, with business getting smarter by tapping the collective brainpower of community.

Company Index

Name Index

Subject Index

Acknowledgments

Since the premise of this project was to involve a large number of people in the creative process, writing a brief acknowledgements section is a unique challenge. But the contributions of a small group of people stand out and deserve to be highlighted.

Tim Moore, Vice President at Pearson and Publisher of both Wharton School Publishing and The Financial Times Press, provided discipline when we most needed it—best summed up by his typical refrain, "Hey, folks, we need to get this community up and running and a book from them finished."

Tim and the Pearson team were the project's emotional drivers relying equally on enthusiasm, irritation, and encouragement to keep us moving toward an actual, tangible end product from this groundbreaking social networking project. Tim's prodding and his willingness to view the process as an experiment helped immensely, and we are grateful for his and his team's encouragement and support.

Donna Carpenter and Maurice (Mo) Coyle drove the bulk of the research and the writing which was derived from the community's contributions and from leaders in the social networking market. They are masters of the written word, and their skills are largely what made the contributions of the community so readable and easy for those interested in social networking in their companies to understand. This is not the first book that has benefited from their unique abilities and, we are certain, it will not be their last in partnership with emerging business communities. We deeply appreciate their efforts.

Isaac Hazard had the most difficult job among us—to coordinate the day-to-day activities of the community and all of its constituents. To say he did so with grace and calm would be a gross understatement; a better characterization would be to note that despite the chaos and panic that engulfed a community-oriented project on a regular basis, Isaac kept everyone on track and, somehow, got the community to work as "one"—sharing their collective wisdom with each other. Thank you, Isaac.

Tom Malone from MIT was deeply involved in the design of many aspects of the community, from the approach to offer incentives to the community contributors to the open source license we used to capture the wisdom of the community. He brought an academic's discipline to the discussion, and reminded us that we were engaged not only to publish a book but to experiment with a process that was unique and groundbreaking. His questions and ideas significantly strengthened the initiative, for which we are grateful.

Jerry Wind from The Wharton School supported this community initiative from its earliest days, and we are proud to publish this book under the Wharton School Publishing banner. Jerry has an extraordinary ability to see value in ideas from their earliest stage of conception, but also to add value to those ideas at every stage of development. His contributions are much appreciated especially during the most difficult moments.

Finally, we are indebted to a group of people we have never met, and who—as far as we know—have never met each other. Ten individuals from our community volunteered to be "chapter leaders" to help monitor and guide the discussion of various chapters in the book. They did so when the role of chapter leader was largely undefined, and they performed their role ably and without compensation or (until now) recognition: Lilly Evans, Ryan Mykita, Greg Krauska, Margot Sayers, Olivier Amprimo, Joe Flumerfelt, Rich Luker, Bruce Hazard, Mel Aclaro, and Rui Monteiroour deepest thanks. The project could not have proceeded without you.

We were also ably assisted by a tremendous team. Many thanks to:

Shared Insights

Michael Libert	Jim Storer
Isaac Hazard	Gary Bellardino
Charlotte Daher	Aaron Strout
Robin Rose	Erika Halloran
Joe Tremonte	Mark Wallace
Shanon Mckenna	Chris Edwards
Shannon Di Gregorio	Stephen Marcus
Mia Encarnacion	

Marketing, PR, and Design

Peter Himler	Mark Fortier
Giles Dickerson	

Pearson

Tim Moore	Amy Neidlinger
Pamela Boland	Russ Hall
Julie Phifer	Amy Fandrei
Megan Colvin	Gina Kanouse
Kristy Hart	Cheryl Lenser
Jake McFarland	Dan Uhrig

Wharton

Carol Orenstein	Yoram (Jerry) Wind
Tracy Simon	Matt Schuler

Wordworks

Donna Carpenter	Maurice Coyle
Ruth Hlavacek	Larry Martz
Cindy Butler Sammons	Robert W. Stock

MIT

Thomas Malone	Stephen Buckley
Sean Brown	Paul Denning
Tammy Cupples	

Legal

Scott Soloway	Karen Rivard

Chapter Moderators

Lilly Evans	Ryan Mykita
Greg Krauska	Margot Sayers
Olivier Amprimo	Joe Flumerfelt
Rich Luker	Bruce Hazard
Mel Aclaro	Rui Monteiro

Board Advisors

Philip Evans	Jimmy Wales

The Helen Rees Literary Agency

Helen Rees	Joan Mazmanian

Joseph Krueger • john Kruper • Agnieszka Krzeminska • Piotr Kubiaczyk • Sean Kubin • Michael Kugler • John Kuijpers • Eugene Kujawa • Bernd Kulawik • Chaitanya Kulkarni • manish kulkarni • Nirupama Kulkarni • Linda Kulp • Ashish Kumar • Dinesh Kumar • Jitender Kumar • Kamlesh Kumar • Krishna Kumar • Kumar Kumar • Kumar • Namith Kumar • NIRAJ KUMAR • Raj Kumar • Sandeep Kumar • Shiva Kumar • Uplaksh Kumar • Vilasini Kumar • Vicki Kung • Abhijeet Kunte • Allen Kupetz • Takahiro Kurachi • Mark Kurtz • Priti Kurtz • Monika Kurzawa • Abhilash Kushwaha • Olha Kutsevych • Joshua Kutticherry • Kazumi Kuwahara • Kyle Kuypers • Subrahmanyam KVJ • Beth L • mike l Sivalingam L • David L. Smith • Ed LaBanca • Alberto Labarga • Christian Labezin • Cynthia LaConte • Dena Ladner • Bruce LaDuke • Ira Laefsky • Stephen Lahey • Jacqueline Lai • Benjamin Laimon • Ron Laing • Vijay Lakshman • Srinivasa Raghavan Lalapet • Ashok Lalla • Stuart Lally • Maurice Lam • Robert Lam • Robin Lamb • Patrick Lambe Rubens Lamel • Jonas Lamis • Bert Lancaster • Dottie Lancaster • Valerie Landau • Hanne Landbeck • Jonathan Landgrebe • Maggie Landis • Barbara Landon • Thomas Landschof • Daisy Landvik • Eva Lang • Lynn Lang • D Terence Langendoen • Ronald Langevin • Karen Langlie • Carlene Lanier • Todd Lappin • Michael Laric • Daniel Larimer • Don Lariviere • Joan Larkin • Christine Larsen • Laura Larson-Huffaker • Matt Lasater • Burke LaShell • Peter Lasinger • Hannah Latham • Milan Lathia • Katherine Lato • Albert Tsz Ming Lau • Rhett Laubach • Robert Laubacher • Dale Laughlin • Misako Lauritzen • Paul Lavallee • Allexe Law-Flood • Bonnie Lawlor • andy lawrence • Katherine Lawrence • Nick Lawrence • Jessica Layden • Nancy Layne • John Layten • Jeff Lazerus • Karen Leary • Carl Leatherman Jr • Karen Leavitt • Matthew Leavy • Dean LeBaron • Louis Lebbos • Luis Lecanda • Gregory Lechkun • David Ledgerwood • Ann Lee • Cheng Lee • Darren Lee • Ke-Chung Lee • Robert Lee • Seung Lee • Seungjoo Lee • Sungir Lee • Peter Leerskov • craig lefebvre • David L Lehman • Juhani Lehtonen • Daniel Leidl • JUN LEIDO • Alexandra Leigon • Jan Marco Leimeister • Cosimo Leipold • Amy Leis Thomas P. Leisle Jr. • Andre Leitao Botelho • Raphael Leiteritz • Karen Lekowski • Eben Lenderking • Michael Lennon • Carl Lens • Ricardo Lenzi Timm • Louis Leon • charles leonard • David Leonard • Chris Lepard • Catharine Leppert • Alain Lesaffre • Ben Lesh • Ben Lesh • Edison Lestari • Nathan Letourneau • chi chung leung • Joseph Leverich Dennis Leveris • Natalia Levina • Stuart Levine • Peggy LeVora • Todd Levy • Lukasz Lewandowski • Nancy Lewin • Bert Lewis • Marc Lewis • Richard Lewis • Gregory Li • Jia Li • Meng Li • Ning Li • Xiaobei Li • Xiaosong Li • Wilson Li Youn Hing • Adlinna Liang • Tony Liano • Anne Libby • Michael Liberson • Barry Libert • Ellen Libert • hal libert Michael Libert • Joe Lidoski • Bob Ligget • Michael Ligudzinski • Noelle Lim • Edmund Lim • Daniel Limbach • R Lind • David Lindheimer • Dmitry Linkov • Bill Linnane • Erin Linnihan • Jonathan Linowes • Alex Linsker • neal linson • Jaap Linssen • Gaetan Lion • Gail Lipschitz • Luis Gustavo Lira • Christ Lisangan • Suzana Lisanti • Brad Lishman Veronika Litinski • Paul Little • Bruce Liu • sam liu • Juan Livingston • Les Livingstone Ph.D. • Claudio Lo Piccolo • Loy Lobo • ROHAN LOBO • Jim Lockington • Victoria Loewengart • John Loftus • S L Loh • Marcel Loher • Carol Loi • Steven Loi • Rita Loiotile • Mark Lombardi • Kevin Long • Gulshan Longani • Terri Lonier • Brian Loomis • Phi Loomis • Ronaldo Lopes • david lopez • Jared Lopez • Jose Luis Lopez • Enrique Lopez-Gonzalez • Michael Lorenca • Eric Lorup • Julia Loughran • Logan Love • Miriam Love • Tony Lovgren • Simona Lovin • Robert Low • Bruno Lowagie • Eric Lowitt • Rhonda Lowry • Fabian Lua • Jackie Luan • Romero Lubansky • Dale Lucas • John Lucas • Mark Lucas • Ricardo Lucas • Hilda Elina Lucci • Antonio Lucena de Faria • Jeff Luckett • Chris Lucksted • Kevin Luddy • Ruth E Luehr • Manuel Luiz • Stephan Lukac • Zbigniew Lukasiak • Susan Luke • Rich Luker • Jeffery Lumkes • Peter Lundrigan • Lycos Lurker • Kevin Ly • Francis Lynch • Simon Lynch • elena lytkina • Michael Lyu • Thirunavukkarasu M • M Venkatesh M • Zheng Ma • Ron Maas • Joe Mac Donald • Rita Macdonald • James R. MacDonald • Hamish MacEwan • Neil MacIver • Simon Mackenzie • Quentin Mackie • Judy MacLean • Bruce MacMillan • Colin MacMillan • Andrew MacNamara • Kathryn Macomber • Alan MacPhail • Scot MacTaggart • Bruce MacVarish • JACQUI MACY • Satya Devarakonda Madan • Murali Maddala • Tom Maddox • Stewart Mader • Neel Madhvani • Michael Madison • Deanna Maestas • Victor Magdaraog • Susan Magee • Rohit Mahajan • rajagopalan mahalingam • Sameh Maharaj • kishor maharjan • Steve Maher • Sachin Mahishi • John Mahoney • Glenda Maikell • Heather Maitre • Svetozar Majstorovic • Anirban Majumdar • Uttam Majumdar • Steven Mak • Stan MAKARCHUK • Jerry Malec • Meeta Malhotra • Manish Malik • Pushpasish Mallick • Thomas Malone • Janice Maloney • Richard Maltzman • Taylor Mammen • Cesar Mamone • Community Manager • Mickey Mancenido • Mark Mandel • Alexander Mandl • Ralph Manfredo • Chuck Manfredonia • Kalyan Mangalapalli • Paolo Mangiafico • Joan Mangum • Manjari Manjari • Paula Mann • Michael Mannion • Dan Mannisto • Mirko Manojlovic • Michael Manojlovich • Rogerio Manso • SOLEDAD MANZI • Isaac Mao • June Marchand • gustavo marchisone • Yannis Marcou • Bob Marcus • MICHAEL MARCUS • Owen Marcus • Simon Marcus • Stephen Marcus • Nivaldo Tadeu Marcusso • Arcadio marcuzzi • Michael Margolis • Sheila Margolis • tom marini • Danielle Marino • Janna Markle • Micah Markman • Bill Markmann • Erik Markowitz • Christian Marks • jim marks • peter markulis • james marley • ismail marmouth • Leslie Marqua • José Marques • Alexandre Marques dos Santos • nestor marquez • Agustin Marreiros • Greg Marsh • Mike Marsh • Steve Marsh • Bob Marshall • Dr. Edward Marshall • Elisha Marshall • Stephen Marshall • Stewart Marshall • Patrizia Marsura • Robert Martens • Carlos Martí • Birgi Martin • Donald Martin • Joel Martin • Jonna Martin • Mary Jo Martin • Michele Martin • Dave Martindale • Thomas Martine • Jose Martínez • John Martino • Amanda Martin-Palmay • Pedro José Santos Martins • Konrad Marx • John Masanda • Robert Mascarenas • Fabio Masetti • Elliott Masie • Marilyn Mason • Chris Masse • Mick Mather • Paul Mathew • Saurabh Mathur • Samir Matkar • Jonathan Matkowsky • Lyes Matmatte • Jose Matos • Craig Matteson • David Matthews • Nicola Mattina • Mari Mattsson • Caroline Maun • Vincent Maurin • Amelia Maurizio • John May • Robert May • Thomas May • Fernando Maya • Christian Mayaud • Bessie Mayes • Kelly Mayes • mark mayhew • Edward Mazze • Daniele Mazzocchi • Christiane Mazzola • Sam Mbale • mhairi mcalpine • Colin McCall-Peat • Terry McCamish • Brian McCarthy • Diane McCarthy • Douglas McCarthy • Paul McCarthy • John McCauley • marta mccave • Leona McCharles • lynn McCollough • Alan McCord • Phil McCormick • Scott McCormick • Mack McCoy • Joe McCraw • Ellen McCullough • jeff mccullough • s mcd • James McDaniel • Andy McDermott • Richard McDermott • Brian McDonald • Dennis McDonald • Mary McDonald • Julan McDonough • Des McEttrick • Kevin McEvoy • Ken McGaffin • william mcgauley • Carolyn McGibbon • Ray McGlew • Richard McGlynn • James McGovern • Fergal McGrath • Patia McGrath • Sean McGrath • Bill "McGRATH, Ph.D." • James McGregor • Blake McGuire • Ginger McGuire • Robert McIlree • Marta McIlroy • Thaddeus McIlroy • Bob McInnis • Sean McIntyre • Mary McKaig • Jake McKee • Blanca McKelvey • Bill McKenna • Matt McKenna • Shanon McKenna • Shanon McKenna • Shanon McKenna • allan mckeown • William McKibbin • Anne McKinnis • Rich McLafferty • Michael McLaughlin • Drew McLellan • Chelsea McLennan • Freddie McMahon • Brandon McNamara • Ken McNamara • Jeff McNeill • Jacob McNulty • Robert McPherson • catherine mcquaid • Jeff McQuillan • Daniel McShane • Traa Me • Sean Mead • Vince Mease • Julie Medero • Ryan Meffert • girish mehendale • bhavin mehta • Puneet Mehta • Shreejay Mehta • Jim Meier • Kevin Meier • anthony meigides • Raeline Meilak • jeanne Meister • Andreas Meiszner • Stevan Meizlish • yahya melhem • yahya melhem • Charlie Melichar • Greg Meline • Andy Meltzer • Brock Meltzer • Sidney Mendelson • Jose Mendoza • Rodrigo Mendoza Anzures • Leif Meneke • Joao O Menezes • Meredith Mengel • Milan Merhar • Marcel Merola • Bruce Merrifield • jonathan merritt • Michele Merritt • Darlene Meskell • Trevor Messam • Curtis Metz • melissa metz • Andrew Meyer • Patrice Meyers • Bretislav Micek • Stephen Michaele • Dean Michaels • Ron Michalak • Markus Michels • Sergej Middendorp • Prankul Middha • Tom Mierzwa • Bakhtiar Mikhak • p miki • Ron Milam • Gerald Milden • Joe Miles • Joe miles • Matt Miles Scott Miles • Udo Milkau • Bev Millar • Bill Miller • Brett Miller • Joseph Miller • Michael Miller • Michael Miller • Nuno Miller • Patrick Miller • Rex Miller • Ryan Miller • Suzy Miller • Terry Miller • Andreas Milles • John Milner • Andrew Miner • Christine Miner • Patrick Miner • Martin Minnich • Michael Minor • ROBERTO MIRANDA • Abe Mirrashidi • Anil Mishra • Sanjaya Mishra • Rishi Mistry • Christine Mitchell • Ed Mitchell • Joe Mitchell • Lynn Mitchell • Phil Mitchell • Atul Mitra • Arata Mitsumatsu • Navin Mittal • Nitin Mittal • Usman Y. Mobin • Kathrin Moeslein • Sean Moffitt • Joseph Mognon • Armando Moguel y Anza • Mirghani Mohamed • John Mohamed • Michelle Mohr • Michelle Mohr • Kok-Wah Moi • Heng Ngee Mok • Corey Moles • Andrew Molgaard • Matthias Möller • John Molnar • Vicki Momary • Henrique Monnerat • Enrique Monreal • Richard Monson • Haefel • John Monteiro • Rui Pedro Alves Monteiro • S N Mookherjee • Anne Moon • Greg Moon • Seongkeun Moon • Brian Moore • Elisa Moore • Erin Moore • John Moore • John Moore • Roger Moore • Steve Moore • Taylor Moore • Tim Moore • Timothy Moore • Anthony K. Moore • Renee Moorefield • FABIANO MORAIS • Jorge Morales • Lori Moran • Cruz Moreno • Federico Moreno • Toni Moreno • Cole Morgan • Dennis Morgan • James Morgan • Thomas Morgan • Vicki Lynne Morgan • marco morgenstern • Sean Morley • Michel Morneau • Meron Moroz • Colleen Morris • Daniel Morris • jeremy morris • Gordon Morrison • Charles Morrissey • Maurizio Morselli • Lawrence Mortenson • Geoffrey Morton-Haworth • David Mosby • martina moscone • Travis Moses-Westphal • William Mosher • tom moylan • Keerthy Muddahanumaiah • Beth Mueller • Eric Mueller • Bob Muenster • Scott Muglia • Khalid Muhammad • Paras Mukadam • Sandeep Mukherjee • Jean Mulford • John Mullen • mark mullen • christopher muller • Joy Mullett • Kik Mulliner • Atty Mullins • Lynne Mulston • Brian Mulvaney • Melody Mumbauer • Brent Mundy • Charles Munhall • Juan Carlos Munoz Boudeguer • Joyce Munro • CB Murali • JEAN-JACQUES MURAMA • Yoshinori Murano • Kazuyoshi Muroya • Dale We > Me Murphy • Erik Murphy • Jay Murphy • Ryan Murphy • Art Murray • Brian Murray • Karla Murray • Michael Murray • Mary Murrell • ASN MURTHY • Deepak Murthy • Madhav Murti • SK Murugaiyan • dickson musslewhite • Tina Mustachio • Carl Muth • Roger Mutimer • Joram Mwinamo • Stephanie Myara • Lee Myers • Ryan Mykita • Sriram N A • Andrej Nabergoj • Ravi Nadig • Yogesh Nagappa • Yiftach Nagar • Morgan Nagarajan • Vinay Nagaraju • Murli Nagasundaram • Steve Nagel • Rajeev Nagpal • Levine Naidoo • Hemanta Naik • Damu Nair • riyad najada • Tatsuya Nakagawa • Byron Nakano • Kevin Nalty • Myungsoo Nam • SREENIVAS NAMANI • Shuvabrata Nandi • kumar nangea • Adolfo Naranjo • Gonzalo Naranjo • Samira Naranjo • popsi narasimhan • Nanjangud Narendra • Vaishali Naroola • Adriana Narvaez • rajiv narvekar • James Nasser • Andrew Nassir • Enda Nasution • Shobha Nat • Joseph Natale • Ramani Natarajan • Ramesh Natarajan • Ashish Nath • chandra nath • Gerhard Jan Nauta • Cristina Nava • Mark Neely • Iya Nefedov • Kenneth Nelder • Andy Nehl • Greg Neichin • Michelle Neil • James Neilson • Robert Neilson • Trevor Nel • Colleen Nelson • Eric Nelson • Glen-Eric Nelson • Leonard Nelson • Shiba Nemat-Nasser • Kurt Nemes • Daniel Nerezov • Dwayne Nesmith • Greg Ness • jean-patrice netter • mark neumann • Dilli Neupane • michael neuvirth • Oliver Neville • karen new • David Newkirk • Bruce Newman • Kevin Newman • Kathryn Newsome • Floyd Newsum • Daniel Newton • Genevieve Ng • Ana-Maria Nicolae • Georgette Nicolaides • B. Nicolini • Nidu Nidu • mark nieker • Iro Niemi • jesus pablo nieto lopez-sidro • ruben nieuwenhuis • Harkamal Nijjar • Brian Niles • William Nisen • Susan Nittmann • Peter Njiru • henry nobibux • Charles Nobles • Kynan Nossjirwan • Luca Nogara • Katsuya Noguchi • Nuno Nogueira • Ales Nohel • Leslie Nolen • Nayaz Noor • Dan Novak • Kae Novak • Randy Noval • Yael Nowogrodski • Siyabulela Ntutela • Tony Nublado • Kenneth Nuckols • Christie Nudelman • Jon Nugent • fabiano nunes • Chuck Nyren • Simon O' Mahony • Maria O'Donovan • Clare O'Brien • John O'Brien • B.L. Ochman • Ed O'Connell • Shannon OConnor • Albert O'Connor • Andrea O'Connor • marga odahowski • Liam O'Doherty • Sean O'Driscoll • Michael O'Dea • Seyoung Oh • Anurag Ojha • Ken Oka • Donal O'Keefe • Malcolm O'Keeffe • chris okoye • Takashi Okubo • Mikael Olsson • Bill O'Luanaigh • Joanna O'Neil • Patrick O'Neil • Jim O'Neill • Thuan Lip Ong • Caner Onoglu • Kelley O'Patry • Darby Orcutt • Robert O'Regan • Raul Orellano • carol orenstein • bruna ori • Sean O'Riordain • Bill Orr • Benjamin Orthlieb • Alvaro Jose Ortiz Santamaria • Iris Ortner • Lynn R Osborn • Lance E. Osborne • Prof. Dan O'Shea • Ahmed Osman • Michael Oster • Fredrik Osterberg • Anna Owsiany • Ali Ozgenc • Ulises Pabon • Barbara Paciotti • Marc Packard • Suresh Padmanabhan • Mark Page • Lou Paglia • Rajendra Pai • Seema Pai • Larry Paine • Fernando Palacios • Ganapathy Palaniswamy • Luis Palma • Mark Palmer • Nathaniel Palmer • Rali Panchanatham • Nikhil Pande • Krishna Kant Pandey • Rakesh R. Pandey • Sohil Pandya • Vipin Pangeni • frank panhandle • Hector Paniagua • Mark Panttaja • Elizabeth Papp • Vijeesh Papulli • Sridhar Parameshwaran • Siva Parameswaran • Rupa Parekh • Margie Parikh • Suchit Parikh • Hyeon Jin PARK • MIN AH PARK • Wonbae Park • Jacqualin Parker • Kellie Parker • Steve Parks • Gopal Parmeswar • Julie Parr • Michael Parsells • Sundar Parthasarathy • Mike Pascucci • Edna Pasher • Kate Pasicznyk • Matt Pasiewicz • Andrew Passant • Joseph Pasquariello • Vishwas Passi • Tina Pastelero • Lynne Pastor • Jaime Pastrana • ron pat • Brijesh Patel • dhiren patel • Mo Patel • niraj patel • Paresh Patel • Parth Patel • Rod Patershuk • steve paterson • Pradnya Pathak • Henry Patner • Tamara Paton • rui patricio • Tristyn Patrick • keith patterson • Anne Pauker-Kreitzberg • Laura Finnerty Paul • Sarup Paul • VICTOR PAUZA • Bo Pawlik • Steve paxhia • Garry Paxinos • Thomas Payne • Dennis Pearce • Lisa Alexandra Pearo • Milton Pedraza • Laura Pedrick • rylan peery • W.J. Pels • Scott Peluso • Christina Pena • Sergio Peñaloza • Natalie Penney • Catherine Pennington • Ivan Pepeljnak • Marcelo Peralta • Orlando Pereda • David Peregrine-Jones • Joel Pereira • Jason Perez • Jose Perez • luis perez • Giulio Perin • anna perinic • Bradley Perkins • Tamsen Perkins • Judith Perle • Howard Perlmutter • Jason Perron • Dave Perry • John Perry • Tim Perry • Douglas Persson • Aaron Peters • StevenRay Petersen • Dave Peterson • Gregory Peterson • Mark Peterson • Terry Ann Peterson • cindy pettit • Joey Petrosino • Fredrik Pettersson • Christy Pettit • Scott Pevey • Kai Pfox • Rory Pheiffer • Karen Phelan • Jerry Phelps • Darin Phillips • Dr. Bert Phillips • Kent Phillips • LORNA PHILLIPSON • John Philpin • Polona Pibernik • Joe Picard • John Picard • Claudio Piccardo • Nancy Picchi • Piero Leo Piccioli • ARTHUR PICCOLO • Debra Piehl • Pertti Pielismaa • andrea pilati • Venu Pillai • Harish Pillay • Keith Pimental • Sharatchandra Pinapati • Lewis Pinault • Karen Pinegar • Koo Ping Shung • Tom Pipal • J. Norberto Pires • Robert Piret • Costa Pissaris • Michal Piszczek • Chris Pitcheos • Donna Pitteri • Taymar Pixley • Michael Platt • Richard Platt • Georg Pleger • Scott Plocharczyk • Scott Plocharczyk • Henrique Plöger Abreu • Andrew Plumb • Philip Pochoda • Sridhar Poduri • Pierre Poirier • Ravi Pokhriyal • Rick Pollack • paolo polverosi • vadim polyakov • Santiago Pombo • Julio sebastian Ponieman • Shweta Ponnappa • Andrea Pontiggia • Devin Poolman • jakanath pooseker • Ben Pope • Adelle Popolo • George Por • Mitch Posada • Clara Potes-Fellow • Paul Power • Will Powley • Rahul Prabhakar • Adarsh Prabhu • Shrikantha Prabhu • Om Prakash • Jason Pramas • Michael Preiss • Charles Prescott • LeeAnn Prescott • Steve Preston • Javier Preto • Susan Price • Scott Priestley • Scott Prieto • Nola Prieto-Ogar • Theunis Prinsloo • LaVern Pritchard • Joe Procopio • hans pronk • Ralph Protsik • shannon prue • Bis Puhan • Piere Antony Puldo Guerrero • Richard Pulik • Ravindranath Pulivarti • Prabal Purkayastha • Andres Purriños • Harold Putman • Jumanah Qaimari • Tahir Qazi • Eric Quanstrom • Mohammad Jahirul Quayum • Patrick Quinlan • Theresa Quintanilla • Humberto Quinteros • g r • John Raabe • Mike Rabbitte • richard rabins • Muriel Rabu • john racovelli • Kathleen Rader • Raluca Radu • Mohammed Raei • John Raezer • Chitra Raghunath • Keyvan Rahmatian • Reena Rai • Deborah Raines • John Rainford • nitin raizada • Sundara Rajan • Sharath Rajasekar • Kunal Ramaiya • Anantha Ramakrishnan • Arvind Ramakrishnan • Selvanayagam Ramalingam • Hari Ramamurthy • Balasubramanian Ramaswamy • Parvathi Ramesh • Gabriel Ramini • Vanessa Ramos • Shilpa Ramtekkar • Candi Randolph • Prem Ranganath • Rajiv Ranganath • Atul Rangarajan • JP Rangaswami • Shabbir Rangwala • David Rankin • Nayan Ranpura • gayatri rao • Nirmal Rao • Nishant Rao • Rahul Rao • Tushar Rao • labbé raphael • Julie Raptis • Charlie Rasko • Piyush Rastogi • Bharat Rathi • Digvijay Singh Rathore • Raghvendra Rathore • Jayseaar Ratliff • Cecilia Rauek • Ahsan Rauf • Lisa Raufman • yannick rault • Gilad Ravid • Ashwin Ravikumar • Prasad Ravilla • Rahul Rawat • partha pratim ray • Duane Raymond • remaji raynal • John Rea • Timothy Rea • William Reade • Douglas Reay • Allison Reece • Connie Reece • Kathleen Rand Reed • Leslie Reed Shields • Howard Rees • Peter Rees • jessica